I0015652

Raspberry Pi Gaming

Second Edition

Design, create, and play all kinds of video games
on your Raspberry Pi computer

Shea Silverman

BIRMINGHAM - MUMBAI

Raspberry Pi Gaming

Second Edition

First published: September 2013

Second edition: February 2015

Production reference: 1170215

Published by Packt Publishing Ltd.
Livery Place
35 Livery Street
Birmingham B3 2PB, UK.

ISBN 978-1-78439-933-7

www.packtpub.com

Credits

Author

Shea Silverman

Reviewers

Dustin Larmeir

Matt Murray

Harish Pillay

Dan Purdy

Commissioning Editor

Pramila Balan

Acquisition Editor

Owen Roberts

Content Development Editor

Samantha Gonsalves

Technical Editor

Prajakta Mhatre

Copy Editors

Pranjali Chury

Merilyn Pereira

Adithi Shetty

Project Coordinator

Sanchita Mandal

Proofreaders

Simran Bhogal

Linda Morris

Indexer

Mariammal Chettiyar

Production Coordinators

Manu Joseph

Nilesh R. Mohite

Cover Work

Manu Joseph

About the Author

Shea Silverman has been using computers since he was two years old. He has always been drawn to technology, video games, education, and the public sector. He is an employee at the Center for Distributed Learning at UCF, where he spends his time researching and developing new ways to enhance online learning. He is a member of the Orlando makerspace FamiLAB and an alumni of the University of Central Florida. His article entitled *Hacking, Learning, and the Raspberry Pi* was published in *2600: The Hacker Quarterly*, he was a technical reviewer for *Raspberry Pi Networking Cookbook, Packt Publishing*, and is the author of *Raspberry Pi Gaming, Packt Publishing*.

You can find more information about him at `http://www.sheasilverman.com`.

I would like to thank my wonderful wife, Kristene, who provides unending encouragement and support to my projects. I would like to thank my friends and family for their ongoing support, especially my grandma for always believing in me. Finally, I would like to thank Liz, Eben, and the Raspberry Pi Foundation for the creation of the Raspberry Pi, as well as the the wonderful community that has flourished since its release.

About the Reviewers

Dustin Larmeir has worked in the web hosting and cloud industry for nearly 10 years, supporting Linux systems and the virtualization infrastructure. He is an avid technology enthusiast and loves learning new concepts as well as teaching others.

> I'd like to thank my wife for all of her support through the years in my pursuit of a career in technology.

Matt Murray is a creative technologist who loves all things tech, art, and education-related. He holds a bachelor's degree in computer animation and is a self-taught programmer, who started at the age of 14. In more recent years, Matt has been tinkering with more and more hardware-related projects with a hope to help bridge virtual worlds with our own.

> I would like to thank my patient wife and kids.

Harish Pillay has been in the ICT industry for over 30 years. He is currently with Red Hat, working on community-related engagements at the government, corporate, and end developer levels. Harish holds an MSEE and a BSCS, both from Oregon State University. Harish founded the Singapore Linux Users Group in 1993. In 2005, he was inducted into the Council of Outstanding Early Career Engineers by the College of Engineering, Oregon State University. In 2009, he was elevated to Fellow of the Singapore Computer Society. In 2013, he was named Distinguished Partner by SPRING Singapore, the national standards and quality agency in Singapore for his work and contributions to IT standards in Singapore and at the International Standards Organization (ISO).

> Eternal gratitude to my soul mate, Usha, and our two sons, Ajay and Amrish, for their unconditional love and support for all the crazy things that I do.

Dan Purdy is a London-based frontend developer. He graduated from the University of Huddersfield with a degree in music technology and audio systems and then worked as a technical engineer at a top London recording studio, where he helped maintain their vast array of equipment and provided technical assistance on a variety of projects. During this time, he developed and built several web applications to centralize and digitize many of the studios' processes, while also experimenting with Raspberry Pi. He developed several standalone applications and games, ranging from kiosk-style displays and take counters to aid assistants and clients to a barcode reading microphone logging system. Projects are documented, along with tutorials, on his blog at https://www.danpurdy.co.uk.

Dan has since moved on to work as a full-time developer at a digital agency in London, working on enterprise-level web applications, e-commerce sites, and prototypes while continuing to experiment with new frameworks and technologies. He also continues to develop and document new Raspberry Pi projects.

www.PacktPub.com

Support files, eBooks, discount offers, and more

For support files and downloads related to your book, please visit www.PacktPub.com.

Did you know that Packt offers eBook versions of every book published, with PDF and ePub files available? You can upgrade to the eBook version at www.PacktPub.com and as a print book customer, you are entitled to a discount on the eBook copy. Get in touch with us at service@packtpub.com for more details.

At www.PacktPub.com, you can also read a collection of free technical articles, sign up for a range of free newsletters and receive exclusive discounts and offers on Packt books and eBooks.

https://www2.packtpub.com/books/subscription/packtlib

Do you need instant solutions to your IT questions? PacktLib is Packt's online digital book library. Here, you can search, access, and read Packt's entire library of books.

Why subscribe?

- Fully searchable across every book published by Packt
- Copy and paste, print, and bookmark content
- On demand and accessible via a web browser

Free access for Packt account holders

If you have an account with Packt at www.PacktPub.com, you can use this to access PacktLib today and view 9 entirely free books. Simply use your login credentials for immediate access.

Table of Contents

Preface

Hi! Welcome to the wonderful world of the Raspberry Pi. In a few short years, the Raspberry Pi has amassed a rich diversity of software, cultivated by its incredible community.

In this book, we are going to explore the entertainment capabilities of the Raspberry Pi. From programming your own video games, to reliving classic moments with your favorite game systems, I'm positive Raspberry Pi gaming will help you unlock the capabilities of your device.

What this book covers

Chapter 1, Getting Started with the Raspberry Pi, will explain the various differences between the Raspberry Pi models, show you how to set up an SD card for use in your device, and finally how to hook up your Raspberry Pi.

Chapter 2, Scratch, will introduce the programming language and programming concepts required to build a game. By the end of this chapter, you will have made two games reminiscent of Flappy Bird and Ping Pong.

Chapter 3, Raspberry Pi Gaming Operating Systems, guides you through the different operating systems that are dedicated to video gaming. These distributions have been specially set up to offer a fun out-of-the-box experience.

Chapter 4, Emulators, explains the various gaming consoles that are available to be emulated on the Raspberry Pi. You will also learn how to access the Raspberry Pi App Store and use the built-in software repository.

Chapter 5, Ported Games, shows you how to install and use games that were originally for other systems but have now been reprogrammed to run on the Raspberry Pi.

Chapter 6, Linux Games, explores those games that are native to the Linux operating system.

Chapter 7, Controllers, will introduce and explain the world of controllers, gamepads, and arcade sticks, and how they can interface with the Raspberry Pi. You will also learn how to hook up your favorite console game pads to your Pi.

Chapter 8, Troubleshooting, will guide you through the common issues that crop up when utilizing a Raspberry Pi.

Appendix, Games List, provides you with a list of the native Linux games that are available in the Raspbian repositories.

What you need for this book

You will need:

- A Raspberry Pi
- An SD card (4 GB or higher)
- A computer running OS X, Windows, or Linux
- A network connection

Who this book is for

If you are someone who loves to play games and are interested in learning more about the capabilities of your Raspberry Pi, this book is for you. Basic knowledge of Raspberry Pi programming is expected.

Conventions

In this book, you will find a number of text styles that distinguish between different kinds of information. Here are some examples of these styles and an explanation of their meaning.

Code words in text, database table names, folder names, filenames, file extensions, pathnames, dummy URLs, user input, and Twitter handles are shown as follows: "In the command prompt, type `startx` to launch the desktop environment."

When we wish to draw your attention to a particular part of a code block, the relevant lines or items are set in bold:

1. Run `sudo chown pi /opt/retropie/configs/all/retroarch.cfg`.

2. Then run `cd /opt/retropie/emulators/RetroArch/installdir/bin`.

3. Finally, run `sudo ./retroarch-joyconfig -j 0 >> /opt/retropie/configs/all/retroarch.cfg`.

Any command-line input or output is written as follows:

```
mc.setBlock(player.x +1, player.y, player.z, block.GOLD_BLOCK)
```

New terms and **important words** are shown in bold. Words that you see on the screen, for example, in menus or dialog boxes, appear in the text like this: "After clicking on **Connect**, you will be asked to log in as **Registered User** or as **Guest**. Choose **Guest**."

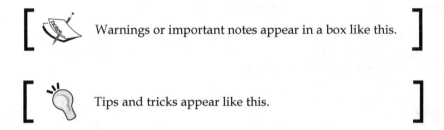

Warnings or important notes appear in a box like this.

Tips and tricks appear like this.

Reader feedback

Feedback from our readers is always welcome. Let us know what you think about this book—what you liked or disliked. Reader feedback is important for us as it helps us develop titles that you will really get the most out of.

To send us general feedback, simply e-mail `feedback@packtpub.com`, and mention the book's title in the subject of your message.

If there is a topic that you have expertise in and you are interested in either writing or contributing to a book, see our author guide at `www.packtpub.com/authors`.

Customer support

Now that you are the proud owner of a Packt book, we have a number of things to help you to get the most from your purchase.

Downloading the color images of this book

We also provide you with a PDF file that has color images of the screenshots/diagrams used in this book. The color images will help you better understand the changes in the output. You can download this file from: `https://www.packtpub.com/sites/default/files/downloads/9337OS_ColoredImages.pdf`.

Errata

Although we have taken every care to ensure the accuracy of our content, mistakes do happen. If you find a mistake in one of our books—maybe a mistake in the text or the code—we would be grateful if you could report this to us. By doing so, you can save other readers from frustration and help us improve subsequent versions of this book. If you find any errata, please report them by visiting `http://www.packtpub.com/submit-errata`, selecting your book, clicking on the **Errata Submission Form** link, and entering the details of your errata. Once your errata are verified, your submission will be accepted and the errata will be uploaded to our website or added to any list of existing errata under the Errata section of that title.

To view the previously submitted errata, go to `https://www.packtpub.com/books/content/support` and enter the name of the book in the search field. The required information will appear under the **Errata** section.

Piracy

Piracy of copyrighted material on the Internet is an ongoing problem across all media. At Packt, we take the protection of our copyright and licenses very seriously. If you come across any illegal copies of our works in any form on the Internet, please provide us with the location address or website name immediately so that we can pursue a remedy.

Please contact us at `copyright@packtpub.com` with a link to the suspected pirated material.

We appreciate your help in protecting our authors and our ability to bring you valuable content.

Questions

If you have a problem with any aspect of this book, you can contact us at `questions@packtpub.com`, and we will do our best to address the problem.

1
Getting Started with the Raspberry Pi

The Raspberry Pi is an inexpensive, feature-rich modern computer created by the Raspberry Pi Foundation. Since the release of the Model B in 2012, the community surrounding the computer has grown, allowing for an incredible amount of projects and software to be created for the device. These range from programming languages, educational applications, hardware prototypes, and of course, video games.

In this chapter, you will learn the following topics:

- The different flavors of a Raspberry Pi
- Setting up an SD card
- Hooking up your Raspberry Pi

The different flavors of a Raspberry Pi

The Raspberry Pi Foundation has released four major models of the Raspberry Pi computer. They the are Model A, Model B, Model B+, and Model A+. The Raspberry Pi's CPU is the Broadcom BCM2835 chip. It contains an ARM processor running at 700 MHz and a powerful graphics chip. The board features HDMI and Composite (RCA) video outputs, USB ports, two expansion slots, a Micro USB port for power, and an array of **GPIO (General-purpose input/output)** pins to interact with the outside world.

Since all models share the same basic hardware platform, all the examples in this book are applicable to all the versions.

	Model A	Model A+	Model B	Model B+
USB	1	1	2	4
Ethernet	0	0	1	1
Video outputs	HDMI/ Composite	HDMI/ Composite via 3.5 mm jack	HDMI/ Composite	HDMI/ Composite via 3.5 mm jack
Memory	256 MB	256 MB	512 MB	512 MB
Storage	SD card	MicroSD card	SD card	MicroSD card
Power usage	300 mA	300 mA	700 mA	600 mA
Price	$25	$20	$35	$35
Differences	Low cost solution. Does not have built in Ethernet and it has only one 1 USB port.	Newest board. Low power, low cost, and much smaller form factor.	Original board. Balances features and price.	New revision to the B board. Has a new layout, 4 USB ports, and more GPIO pins.

Setting up an SD card

The Raspberry Pi uses SD cards to contain its operating system and main storage space. A Raspberry Pi SD card contains two partitions, which are explained as follows:

- The first one, is the boot partition. This space contains the Linux kernel, required boot up files, and most importantly, the config.txt file. This file allows you to change the boot time parameters and customize some of the functions of the Raspberry Pi. These options include over-clocking the device, changing monitor settings, and the memory split between CPU and GPU, among numerous other options.

- The second partition contains a Linux partition, which holds all of your applications, configurations, and operating system files.

Preloaded SD card images are available, which make it quick and easy to get your Raspberry Pi up and running.

Choosing an SD card is an important step. There are many different combinations of card sizes and card speeds. 4 GB is the minimum size required for many of the **operating systems (OS)**. I recommend that you start out with an 8 GB card. You will also see cards marked with Class 4, Class 6, and Class 10. This is the speed at which the card can be read and written to. I have found that the best bang for the buck is a Class 6 card, but don't worry too much about which one you choose.

Before we begin, you will need to download a suitable Raspberry Pi OS. We will be using the official operating system called Raspbian. You can download it from

`http://www.raspberrypi.org/downloads`.

 Warning! dd and Win32DiskImager can be used to overwrite your computer's own hard drive or other drives connected to your computer. Double and triple check that the drive you select is your SD card.

Creating the SD card in Windows

To create the SD card in Windows, you will need to download the program called Win32DiskImager by visiting `http://sourceforge.net/projects/win32diskimager/`.

Once you are done with the downloading, perform the following steps:

1. Unzip the Raspbian image by double-clicking on the `Raspbian.zip` file.
2. Select a place on your hard drive to save the extracted file.
3. Click on **Extract files…**.
4. Insert the SD card into your computer's SD card reader.
5. Run **Win32 Disk Imager**.

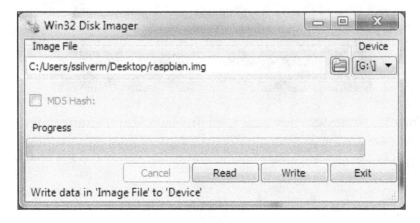

6. Select the Raspberry Pi image on your hard drive.

7. Select the drive letter under the device that corresponds to the SD card.

8. Click on **Write**.

Creating the SD card in Macintosh OS X

OS X includes everything you need to create the SD card out of the box. We will use a utility called dd:

1. Double-click the Raspbian image ZIP file. It will automatically extract into the same place as the ZIP file.

2. Insert the SD card into your computer's SD card reader.

3. Open the terminal application (located in the **Applications | Utilities** folder).

4. Find the name of your SD card by typing `diskutil list`.

```
C02FV3EJDF91:~ shea$ diskutil list
/dev/disk0
   #:                     TYPE NAME              SIZE        IDENTIFIER
   0:     GUID_partition_scheme                 *121.3 GB    disk0
   1:                      EFI                   209.7 MB    disk0s1
   2:         Apple_HFS Macintosh HD             120.5 GB    disk0s2
   3:         Apple_Boot Recovery HD             650.0 MB    disk0s3
/dev/disk1
   #:                     TYPE NAME              SIZE        IDENTIFIER
   0:     GUID_partition_scheme                 *320.1 GB    disk1
   1:                      EFI                   209.7 MB    disk1s1
   2:     Microsoft Basic Data BOOTCAMP          127.7 GB    disk1s2
/dev/disk2
   #:                     TYPE NAME              SIZE        IDENTIFIER
   0:     FDisk_partition_scheme                *2.0 GB      disk2
   1:         Windows_FAT_32 boot                58.7 MB     disk2s1
   2:                    Linux                   1.9 GB      disk2s2
C02FV3EJDF91:~ shea$
```

5. Unmount your SD card by typing `disktuil umountdisk <disk>`, that is, /dev/disk2.

```
C02FV3EJDF91:~ shea$ diskutil umountdisk /dev/disk2
Unmount of all volumes on disk2 was successful
C02FV3EJDF91:~ shea$
```

6. Copy the OS image from your hard drive to the SD card by typing `dd if=/path/to/os/image.img of=<disk>` where `<disk>` is `/dev/disk2`, and `path/to/os/image.img` is the place to which you saved the image.

7. It can take anywhere from 15 minutes to over an hour for the image to be written to the SD card. It will look like nothing is happening until it finishes copying. When it is done, you will see a message showing how long it took to transfer in seconds.

```
C02FV3EJDF91:~ shea$ dd if=/Users/shea/raspbian.img of=/dev/disk2
3788800+0 records in
3788800+0 records out
1939865600 bytes transferred in 1837.087116 secs (1055946 bytes/sec)
C02FV3EJDF91:~ shea$ ▊
```

[You can press *Ctrl* + *T* at any time to see the current status.]

Creating the SD card in Linux

Like OS X, Linux includes everything you need out of the box:

1. Insert the SD card into your computer's SD card reader.

2. Using the terminal of your system, find the name of your SD card by typing `sudo fdisk -l`.

3. If required, you can unmount your SD card by typing `umount <disk>` (which will be listed from the earlier command , `IE/dev/disk2`).

4. Copy the OS image on your hard drive to the SD card by typing `dd if=/path/to/os/image.img of=<disk>`.

Now that you have created your Raspberry Pi SD card, it's time to set up our device!

Using NOOBS

The Raspberry Pi Foundation has created a piece of software called **New Out Of the Box Software**, often abbreviated as **NOOBS**. This is a small operating system, which is used to install other OSs onto your Raspberry Pi.

Installing NOOBS is much easier than other installs:

1. Download NOOBS from `http://www.raspberrypi.org/downloads` and unzip the file.

2. Insert the SD card into your computer's SD card reader.

3. Drag and drop the NOOBS files onto the SD card and you are done!

At the first boot, you will be presented with a list of OSs available to be installed. Choose **Raspbian** and press *Enter*.

Hooking up your Raspberry Pi

It's very easy to properly set up a Raspberry Pi. If you can build a Lego set, you can build your Raspberry Pi computer. The following steps will help you in this:

1. Place your SD card into the SD card slot on the underside of the Raspberry Pi.

2. Connect the HDMI or RCA cable to the respective connector on the Raspberry Pi, and plug the other end into your monitor.

3. Plug the Ethernet cable into the Ethernet jack (not applicable to Model A and A+) on the Raspberry Pi and the other end into your router or switch.

4. Connect the USB mouse and keyboard to the two USB ports available on the Raspberry Pi. If you are using Model A, connect a USB hub to your Raspberry Pi and the mouse and keyboard to the hub.

5. Plug the power supply's Micro USB connector into the Micro USB port on the Raspberry Pi to turn it on.

6. A red LED, by the USB ports, will light up to indicate that the power is turned on.

7. On your screen, a square rainbow image will appear for a brief moment, followed by some quick moving text or a graphic loading screen.

Congratulations! You have successfully booted up your Raspberry Pi!

Connecting to a Wi-Fi access point

The Raspberry Pi and Raspbian can easily connect to the Internet via Ethernet, but when using a USB wireless device, you can also connect to a Wi-Fi network. Raspbian includes a graphical utility to make connecting to a Wi-Fi access point easy. Go through the following steps:

1. Boot up your Raspberry Pi.

2. At the login screen, enter your username and password (default is `pi` and `raspberry`, respectively).

3. In the command prompt, type `startx` to launch the desktop environment.

4. Using your mouse, double-click on the **WiFi Config** icon that is on the desktop.

5. The Wi-Fi configuration tool will appear shortly.

6. Click on **Scan** to scan for available wireless networks around you.

7. Double-click on the one you wish to connect to.

8. If it is a secured network, you will be asked for a password.

9. Enter the password and click on **Add**.

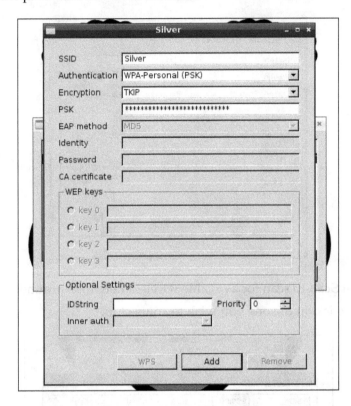

10. The **Status: Disconnected** message should now change to **Status: Completed**.

11. You are now connected to your wireless network.

wpa_gui saves your connection information. If you logout or reboot your Raspberry Pi, it will automatically try to connect to a previously added access point.

If you do not see **wlan0** appear in the **wpa_gui**, or if your Raspberry Pi is unstable, you might need to use a powered USB hub. You should connect your device to a powered hub, and then connect the hub to the Raspberry Pi. This will ensure that the correct amount of power is received.

You can also check whether your Wi-Fi adapter is supported by visiting http://elinux.org/RPi_USB_Wi-Fi_Adapters.

Summary

In this chapter, you learned how to create your Raspberry Pi's SD card, hook it up to your TV and other accessories, and connect it to the Internet. Now, it's time to have fun with the software on your Raspberry Pi.

In the next chapter, you will learn how to create your own video game using the Scratch programming language.

2
Scratch

This chapter will introduce you to the amazing and fun world of programming. Learning to program and code will allow you to bring your ideas to creation. If you have ever wanted to make a game, but had no idea where to start, this is the place.

In this chapter, you will learn the basics needed to make your own video game on the Raspberry Pi. You will learn how to:

- Launch Scratch
- Define your game's objectives
- Draw a character
- Make your character interact and move
- Design and program a Flappy Bird-style game
- Design and create a 2 player Ping Pong game

What is Scratch?

Scratch is a programming language and application developed by the Massachusetts Institute of Technology (MIT) as an easy-to-use, educational, and fun environment to learn to code and to make video games and applications. It is different from most other programming languages. It is completely visual; rather than typing out lines of code, all you have to do is drag and drop visual blocks to create your program.

Games that might have taken days to be created earlier can be created in minutes, right in front of your eyes. Now, you are going to create some games too!

Understanding the Scratch interface

Before we begin writing our first game, you need to understand the Scratch interface. Scratch is not only a powerful programming language, but also a full-featured application. To write Scratch programs use the following steps:

1. Open the Scratch application. This is included on all copies of the official Raspberry Pi operating system, Raspbian.

2. In the command line, type startx to activate the desktop environment.

3. Once at the desktop, double-click on the **Scratch** icon.

4. Scratch should now open and display a brand new project, which is ready for you to begin.

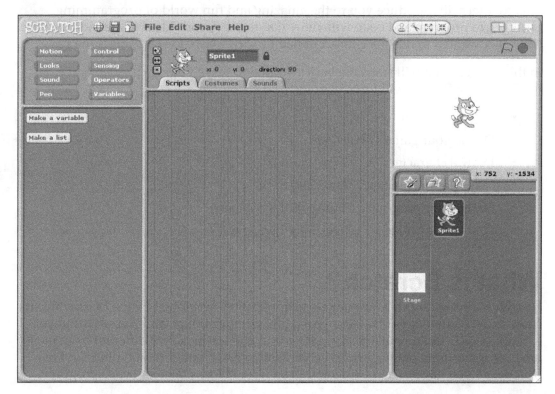

The first things you will notice is that there are three columns. On the far right side, you should see a white square with a happy looking cat. His name is Scratchy. He is also the mascot of Scratch. This panel is where all the action takes place. This is your game screen.

The column in the middle is where all your code will be placed. At the moment there is nothing in here, but this will soon change.

The left column contains every single available command in the Scratch language. To use one of these pieces of code, just click on one and drag it to the middle column.

For our first example, we will make Scratchy move.

Making Scratchy move

Let's get ready to create our first program:

1. Click on Scratchy in the white panel to make sure he is selected. You will see **Sprite1** highlighted in the panel below. Sprites are what these characters are called in Scratch.

2. Now, click on the **Control** button from the left side in the first column.

3. Click on the **When <green flag> clicked** item and drag it to the middle column.

4. Next, click on **Motion** and drag the **move 10 steps** item to the middle column.

5. Move it under the **When <green flag> clicked** until a white line appears between them, and then let go of the mouse button.

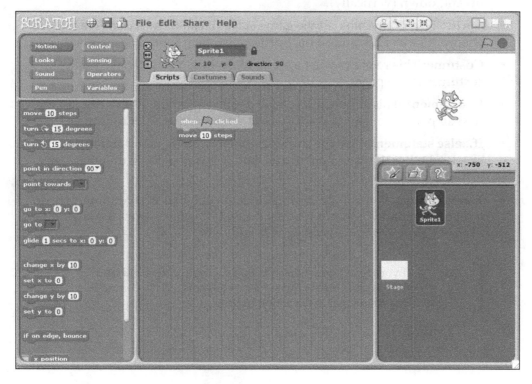

6. Now, click on the green flag button above the game panel, and you should see Scratchy move a bit.

Congratulations! You have just made your first application in Scratch. Let's get ready to make our first game!

Some pointers and terminology

Before we start working on our awesome, exciting, and fun games, here are a few pointers and tips for working with Scratch:

- **Variable**: You can think of a variable as a box that can store things. In Scratch, each variable can store an item, be it a number, a name, or some other value.

- **Stage**: This is the background of the game window. You can set the stage background to be a number of different images, and even include scripts on the stage.

- **X position**: This is where a sprite is on the *x* axis of the stage. The *x* axis goes left and right (horizontally).

- **Y Position**: This is where a sprite is on the *y* axis of the stage. The *y* axis goes up and down (vertically).

- **Sprite**: This is anything on the game stage. It can be a character, a wall, an enemy, a power up, and so on. Sprites have their own costumes and code.

- **Costume**: This refers to what a sprite looks like. You can have multiple costumes for a sprite.

- **If statement**: This simply asks a true or false question. If it's `true`, do the next step. A statement that says `2 = 2` which is true, so it continues.

- **If...else statement**: Like the earlier command, an if...else statement will check whether the statement is true, and if it is not, it will do whatever is in the else block.

- **Forever loops**: Forever loops are blocks of code that will continuously do a set of commands. Once it reaches the end, it restarts from the beginning of the block and performs them over and over.

[If you don't know where to find the right command from the example instructions, look at the color of the command. The colors match the action buttons.]

Let's build a Flappy Bird clone!

Your first game is going to be a Flappy Bird clone. While this might seem like a complicated task, it really can be broken down to a few easy scripts.

 Flappy Bird is a great starting game. It has a clear objective, uses much of the Scratch functionality, is relatively simple to create, and you can use your imagination by drawing your own sprites, backgrounds, and pipes.

What kind of a game is Flappy Bird? It is a game where your goal is to keep on pressing a button to make a bird rise as it is constantly falling while navigating its way through the pipes of varying heights that are coming at it.

It can be broken down as follows:

- Every button press makes the bird go up on the y axis
- Every second the button isn't pressed the bird goes down the y axis
- A pipe starts at the right end of the x axis and moves left toward the bird
- When the pipe reaches the far left corner without touching the bird, you earn a point and the pipe disappears
- If the bird touches the ground or the pipe, then the game is over

So, now we know we need a minimum of two sprites: a bird and a pipe.

What else will we need? We will need a background, a floor, some variables, and a few costumes.

Creating a new project

Before we begin, let's create a new project for our Flappy Bird clone. To do so, click on the **File** menu and then click on **New**. A brand new Scratch project will appear.

Making the variables

Now that we know what we need, we can start by creating our variables:

1. Click on the **Variables** button, and then click on **Make a variable**. It will ask you for a name, and display two options: **For all sprites** and **For this sprite only**. Ensure that you click on **For all sprites**.

2. Our first variable will be named score. Type this and click on **OK**. The score variable will be used to keep track of how many walls you have passed. It will go up by one each time.

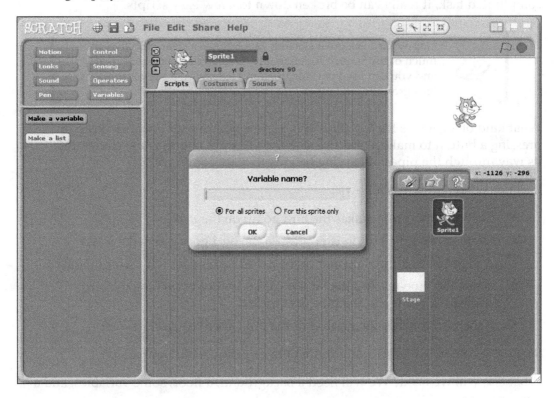

Now, make three more variables with the following names:

- scroll: This will be used to keep track of where the floor is, since it will be moving
- time: This will keep track of how many seconds have passed since you started the game
- pipeX: This will keep track of where the pipe is across the screen

Setting the stage

With our variables created, it is now time to create our game's backgrounds using the following steps:

1. Click on **Stage** in the right column, and then click on **Backgrounds**.

2. Click on **Edit**. You will now be in **Paint Editor**.

3. Click on a color, then the paint can (fill tool), and click anywhere on the white area. Then click on **OK**. You have now changed the background of your game.

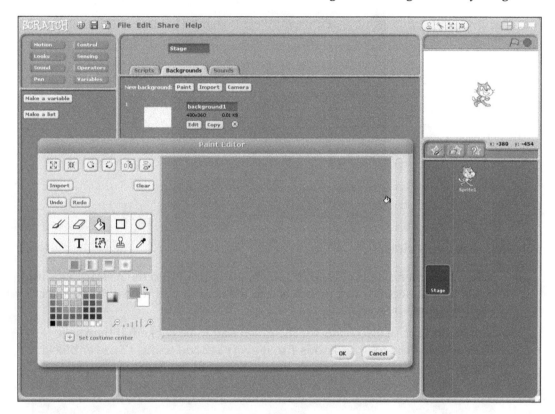

4. Click on **Copy** three times, and then edit each background to be a different color.

5. Now, click on **Scripts**. We will add the first scripts to our game.

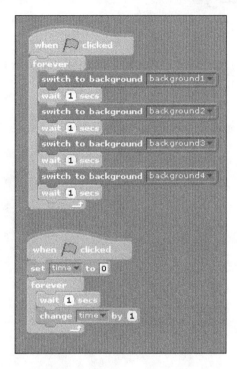

This stage has two scripts:

- When the green flag is clicked, it sets the background to the next background, waits for one second, and then sets it to the next. It will repeat this forever until the game is over.

- The second script also waits for the green flag to be clicked. It then sets the variable time to 0, and adds 1 to it every second using a forever block. The forever block repeats what's inside of it until the game is stopped.

If you click on the green flag, you should see the background change. Now would be a good time to save your game as well. Click on **File**, then choose **Save**. Give your game a name and click on **OK**.

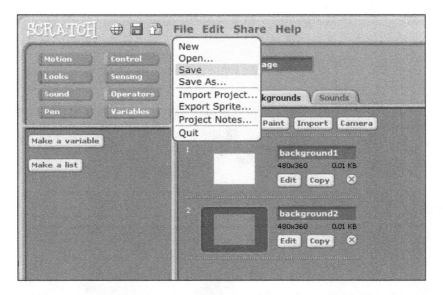

Making the floor

The floor of the game serves two purposes. The first, is to make it look like you are moving because the floor scrolls across the stage. The second, is to be an avoidable object. If you touch the floor, the game is over. Our floor is actually going to be two sprites.

Let's start with the first one:

1. On the right-hand side of the window is an option to create a new sprite. You have three options: **Paint new sprite**, **Choose new sprite from file**, or **Get a surprise sprite**.

2. Create a new sprite by clicking on the **Paint new sprite** button.

3. Now, use the line tool $\boxed{\diagdown}$ and draw a line all the way from the left to the right. Then fill it in with a color using the bucket tool $\boxed{\diagup}$.

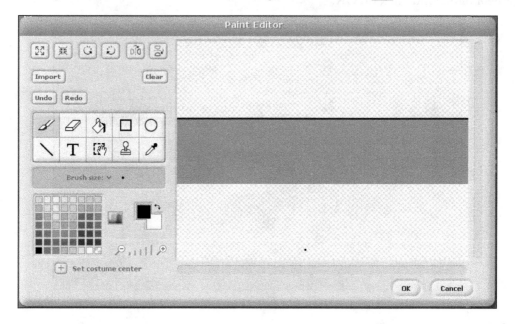

4. Click on **OK**. Name your sprite `Floor1` by clicking on the name textbox in the middle column.

Now, let's create the scripts as follows:

The first floor sprite has three scripts:

- The first script sets the scroll variable to 0, and then until the game is over, it decreases by 1.

- The second script puts the floor into position. After setting the floor to be the front-most item, it sets the y position to -180. This puts it at the bottom of the stage. It then sets the x position of the floor to the current value of the scroll variable. This will make it move.

  ° You will initially drag the **set x to 0** motion to the scripts column.

  ° You will then drag the variable **scroll** over the **0** to change it.

- The third script resets the scroll variable to 0 if it reaches the end of the screen.

Press the green flag button to watch the floor scroll. It seems like there's a small problem though: the floor isn't long enough. It scrolls off the screen with nothing behind it until it reaches the end. Don't worry though. It's a simple fix!

1. Right-click on **Floor1** and then click on **Duplicate**.

2. You should now have a complete copy of your floor sprite. You should rename it to Floor2. Now, click on it and choose **Scripts**. We have to make a few adjustments.

3. Delete the first and third script from Floor2. You can do this by clicking and dragging them to the first (leftmost) column.

4. Now, edit the remaining script to look like this:

By setting x to **scroll + 480**, you will now have a second floor that follows the first floor and continually repeats.

You can add some color and some grass to the costume to add to the scrolling effect.

Creating the pipes

The pipes are relatively straightforward. It is one sprite, with three costumes, and one script to make it scroll across the screen.

1. Click on **Create new sprite** and draw a pipe. Mine is just a long black rectangle going all the way from the bottom to the top of the editor.

2. Use the rectangle tool to select a portion of the pipe and press *Delete*. You now have the area to fly through.

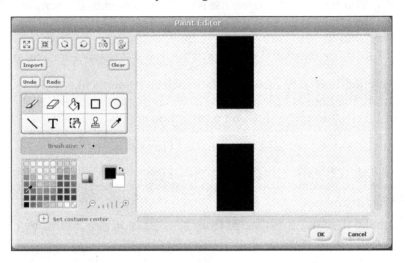

3. Copy the costume two more times. This time refill in the hole and create a new one at a different spot in the pipe.

Now, let's make the pipe scripts!

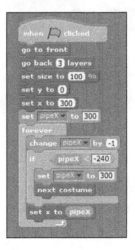

The following steps explain the making of pipe scripts:

1. When the green flag is clicked, move the pipe to the top of the layer, and then back three layers. This will make it appear behind the floor.

2. The set size is a new command. This allows you to make the sprite bigger or smaller. Experiment with the size until you are happy with how it looks. You can also change this to affect the difficulty of the game. If you don't see the hole in the middle of the wall, it maybe because the size is set too high.

3. Then, set *y* to 0, which puts the wall right in the middle of the screen, and *x* to 300, which moves it off the screen to the right.

4. Set the *pipeX* variable to 300. We will use that variable later.

5. In our forever loop, subtract 1 from *pipeX*. Then check whether *pipeX* is less than -240. This allows us to check where it is on the screen. If it is less than -240 (which puts the pipe to the left of the screen), reset the position of the pipe to the far right, by setting *pipeX* back to 300. Then, change the costume to the next one.

6. Finally, set the *x* position of the pipe to pipeX. We now have a scrolling pipe!

Working with the main character

Now, it's time to make our main character! This sprite is going to need two costumes: one with the wings up and one with the wings down. Luckily, Scratch already includes costumes, so you don't have to draw it yourself (but feel free to do so if you want!).

1. If you haven't removed Scratchy yet, right-click on the Scratchy sprite icon in the right column, and select **delete**.

2. Under the game stage, you'll see the **Choose new sprite from file** option. Click on that option.

3. A pop up will be displayed showing a list of folders; choose the folder **Animals**.

4. For my example, I choose **bat1-a** as shown in the following screenshot:

5. Double-click on it, and you will see it appear on your stage and in the sprite panel. Select it, and then click on **Costumes**.

6. Next, in **New costume**, select **Import** and choose **bat1-b**. Your sprite now has the costumes that it needs to look like it's flying.

7. If you feel like drawing your own costume for your sprite, select **Paint** instead.

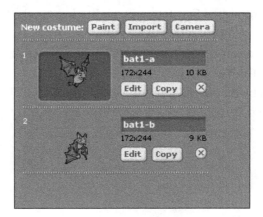

Now, let's work on the scripts for our bat!

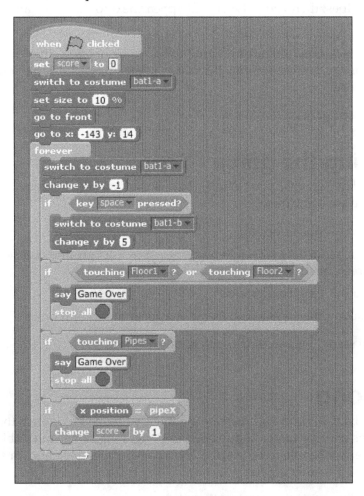

When the green flag is clicked, set the score variable to 0, switch to the costume with the bat wings up, set the size to be 10 percent of the original sprite size, go to the topmost layer, and then move to those *x* and *y* positions. Play around by changing the size of your bat and experimenting with the *x* and *y* positions. Changing these will affect the difficulty of your game.

Now, we enter our forever loop. Each time this loop occurs, we set the sprite to be the bat with wings up, and move it down by 1 on the stage. This next block introduces us to user input. It says that if the space key is pressed on your keyboard, then it should switch to the bat with wings down and move up the stage by 5. You can change the key to be anything on your keyboard. You can also change the 5 to increase or decrease the height at which the bat flies per button press.

The next two `if` blocks follow the same formula. If your bat sprite touches Floor1, Floor2, or the pipes, then **Game Over** will appear next to the sprite and the game will stop.

Finally, if the x position of the bat is equal to the value of *pipeX*, then you should change the score by `1`, since it indicates that you have passed through one of the pipes successfully.

Now, try out your game!

Enhancing the game

Now that you have created your Flappy Bird clone, you should try to enhance and modify it. Here are some ideas:

- Add a multiplayer option
- Create a game over screen by making a new background and setting it to the screen that appears when you touch a pipe
- Make a scrolling background
- Try making the pipes scroll faster or appear at random times

When you are ready, we can move onto the next game.

Ping Pong

It's time to go back in time, and recreate a game that helped to launch the video game industry. It has gone by many names such as Pong, Ping Pong, and Table Tennis, but the basic gameplay has stayed the same. Two paddles, one ball, and an epic battle to get the ball past the other player.

So, let's break down this game. We will require:

- One paddle for the left player
- One paddle for the right player
- One bouncing ball
- Two variables to keep score for each player.

Let's get started!

Making the paddles

After creating a new project, you will be presented with the white stage and a Scratchy sprite.

1. Right-click on Scratchy and click on **delete**. Now, click on **Paint new sprite**.

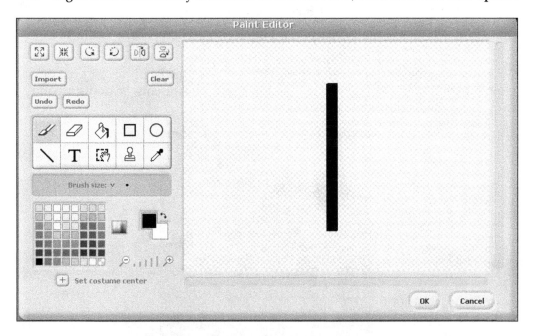

2. Draw a long black rectangle and click on **OK**. Name this sprite Left.

    We are going to create three simple scripts for this paddle, as follows:

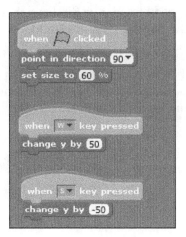

3. The first script ensures that the left paddle points in the proper direction and then sets its size to 60 percent. You should experiment with the size to determine what feels right for your game.

4. The next two scripts control the vertical movement of the left paddle. Again, experiment with the amount of movement that each button press does to change the difficulty of your game.

5. When you have set these up, right-click on your left paddle sprite and click on **Duplicate**.

6. Rename the new sprite to Right. We now have the beginning for making our right paddle. You will be making a few adjustments, so that a second player will control the paddle.

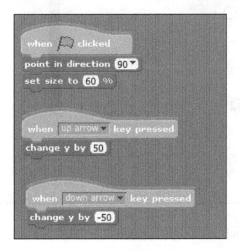

We change the direction in which the paddle is pointing to ensure that it faces the right direction. You then need to change the keys that you will be using for the second player to move the paddle up and down. In this example, we use the up and down arrow keys.

On the stage itself, drag and drop your paddles into the proper positions. The left paddle should be on the left-hand side of the stage, but not touching the wall, while the right paddle should be on the right-hand side, while also leaving a gap between the paddle and the wall.

When you have made your choices, click on the green flag button and test your game. The paddles should be able to move up and down.

Following the bouncing ball

Now, it's time to create the heart of the program: the ball!

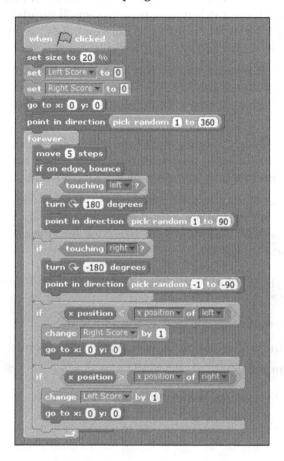

To get started, let's create a new sprite:

1. Start by importing a sprite from the library. There are numerous round ball-like costumes to choose from. When you are happy with your costume, double-click on it. Rename your new sprite to `Ball`.

2. Now, you will need to make two variables. Name them `Left Score` and `Right Score` and set them to be used by all sprites.

3. When the green flag is clicked, set the size of the ball to `20` percent, and set both left score and right score to `0`.

4. Move the ball to the center of the screen, and use a new block to point the ball in a random direction. Random numbers are like picking a number out of a hat. You don't know which one you will get ahead of time. Using a random block, we can give Scratch two numbers, a small number and a large number, and it will pick a random number in between these. By making the ball point in a random direction, we add to the challenge and skill level of the game.

5. Now, onto the forever block. Each time it loops, we want to move the ball 5 steps. We now have another new block, *If on edge, bounce*. This block tells the ball that if it has touched the outer edges of the screen, it should bounce away from it.

6. We now have two `if` statements. These come into effect if the ball touches either the left or the right paddle. If it touches either, we have the ball point in the opposite direction, and then pick a random direction to move in.

7. The last two `if` statements are the most important ones. These check whether the ball has gone behind either of the paddles. If it has, it awards a point to the other paddle, and moves the ball back into the middle of the stage. The game then continues!

You now have the beginning of your Ping Pong game! Where can you go from here? Here are a few ideas:

- Add a background that represents a tennis match.
- Have the game end when one side scores enough points.
- Have the computer play as one of the paddles.

The rest is up to you! Have fun and experiment!

Summary

In this chapter, you learned how to start Scratch, create characters, design, and program two fun games. You have only scratched the surface of what is possible with the Scratch programming language.

While making games is a lot of fun, sometimes you might need to play some for inspiration. Luckily, the Raspberry Pi has some great games and emulators available. The next chapter will introduce you to distributions made just for gaming.

3
Raspberry Pi Gaming Operating Systems

The Raspberry Pi, while a powerful little device, is nothing without software to run on it. Setting up emulators, games, and an operating system can be a daunting task for those who are new to using Linux. Luckily, there are distributions (operating system images) that handle all of this for us. In this chapter, we will demonstrate three distributions that have been specially made for gaming.

In this chapter, you will learn:

- Where to download multiple gaming operating systems from
- Similarities and differences between PiPlay, RetroPie, and ChameleonPi
- How to access Raspberry Pi's shared folders on your computer
- Copying and uploading game files to your Raspberry Pi

PiPlay

PiPlay is an open source premade distribution that combines numerous emulators, games, and a custom frontend that serves as the GUI for the Raspberry Pi. Created in 2012, PiPlay started as PiMAME. Originally, PiMAME was a version of Raspbian that included the AdvanceMAME and AdvanceMENU frontend. The distribution was set to autologin and start up AdvanceMENU at boot up. This project was founded because of the numerous issues users were facing to get MAME to compile and run on their own devices. As more and more emulators were released, PiMAME began to include them in the image, and changed its name to PiPlay, as it wasn't just for arcade emulation anymore.

Currently, PiPlay contains the following emulators and games:

- AdvanceMAME (Arcade)
- MAME4ALL (Arcade)
- Final Burn Alpha (Capcom and Neo Geo)
- PCSX_ReARMed (PlayStation)
- Dgen (Genesis)
- SNES9x (Super Nintendo)
- FCEUX (NES)
- Gearboy (Gameboy)
- GPSP (Gameboy Advance)
- ScummVM (point-and-click games)
- Stella (Atari 2600)
- NXEngine (Cave Story)
- VICE (Commodore 64)
- Mednafen (Game Gear, Neo Geo Pocket Color, Sega Master System, Turbo Grafx 16/PC-Engine)

To download the latest version of PiPlay, go to `http://piplay.org` and click on the **Download** option. Follow the directions from *Chapter 1, Getting Started with the Raspberry Pi*, to burn the PiPlay image to your SD card. When this is completed, insert the SD card into your Raspberry Pi and turn it on.

Within a few moments, you should see an image like this on your screen:

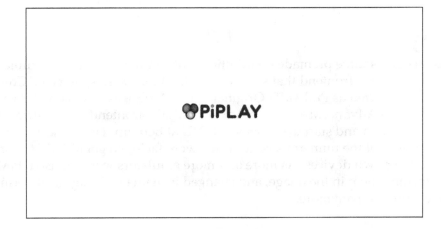

Once it's finished booting, you will be presented with the PiPlay menu screen:

Here, you will see all the different emulators and tools you have available. PiPlay includes an extensive controller setup tool. By pressing *Tab* key or button 3 on your controller, a popup window will appear. Select **Controller Setup** and follow the onscreen guide to properly configure your controller:

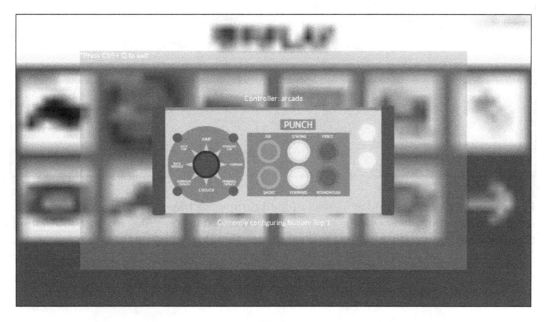

At the moment, there isn't much to do because you haven't loaded any games for the emulators. The easiest way to load your game files into PiPlay is to use the web frontend. If you connect your Pi to your network, an IP address should appear at the top right of your screen. Another way to find out your IP address is by running the command `ifconfig` on the command line.

Navigate your computer's web browser to this address, and the PiPlay frontend will appear:

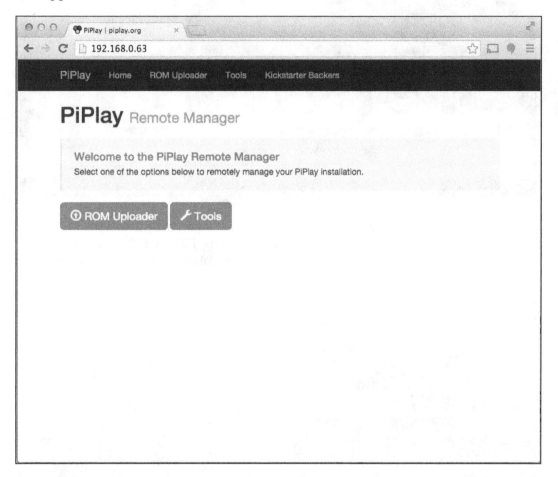

Here, you can reboot, shutdown, and upload numerous files to the Pi via a drag and drop interface. Simply select the emulator you want to upload files to, find your game file, and drag it onto the box. In a few moments, the file will be uploaded.

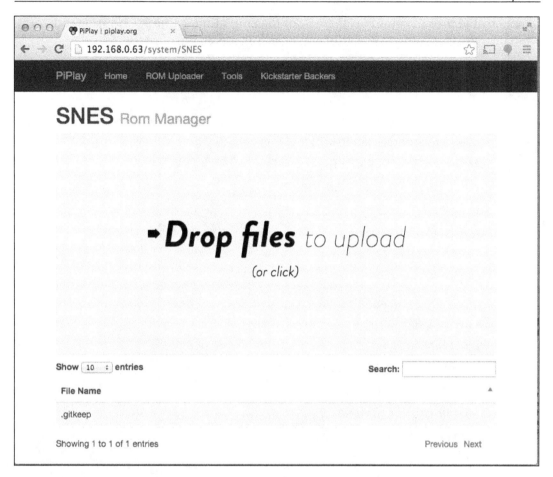

RetroPie

RetroPie is a project based on Libretro, RetroArch, and EmulationStation. EmulationStation is an open source frontend that makes it easy to manage over 30 video game consoles and applications, and your associated game files. It includes a built-in joystick setup tool and can automatically download associated metadata for your files. This metadata includes items such as box art and game info, which gives your collection a polished finish.

Libretro is another open source project. It is designed to bring multiple emulators into one main package. Instead of having a separate application for each system, Libretro turns these emulators into a core, which hooks into the library. By having a common library for each emulator to hook into, a cohesive easy-to-use platform is created for the user. RetroArch is the main frontend for the Libretro library.

The RetroPie project combines the best of the emulation, gaming, and frontend systems into an easy-to-use platform for the Raspberry Pi.

RetroPie includes all of these systems and consoles:

- Amiga (UAE4All)
- Apple II (LinApple)
- Apple Macintosh (Basilisk II)
- Armstrad CPC (CPC4RPi)
- Arcade (PiFBA, Mame4All-RPi)
- Atari 800
- Atari 2600 (RetroArch)
- Atari ST/STE/TT/Falcon
- C64 (VICE)
- CaveStory (NXEngine)
- Doom (RetroArch)
- Duke Nukem 3D
- Final Burn Alpha (RetroArch)
- Game Boy Advance (gpSP)
- Game Boy Color (RetroArch)
- Game Gear (Osmose)
- Intellivision (RetroArch)
- MAME (RetroArch)
- MAME (AdvMAME)
- NeoGeo (GnGeo)
- NeoGeo (Genesis-GX, RetroArch)
- Sega Master System (Osmose)
- Sega Megadrive/Genesis (DGEN, Picodrive)
- Sega Mega-CD (Picodrive)
- Sega 32X (Picodrive)
- Nintendo Entertainment System (RetroArch)
- N64 (Mupen64Plus-RPi)
- PC Engine / Turbo Grafx 16 (RetroArch)

- Playstation 1 (RetroArch)
- ScummVM
- Super Nintendo Entertainment System (RetroArch, PiSNES, SNES-Rpi)
- Sinclair ZX Spectrum (Fuse)
- PC/x86 (rpix86)
- Z Machine emulator (Frotz)

RetroPie is hosted at `http://blog.petrockblock.com/retropie/`. The RetroPie forums, blog, and additional information are also available here. Once you have downloaded the SD card image, follow the instructions in *Chapter 1, Getting Started with the Raspberry Pi*, to move it to your SD card. A few moments after booting up your Raspberry Pi, you should be presented with a screen similar to the following:

After the Raspberry Pi has finished booting up, you will be presented with the EmulationStation splash screen:

RetroPie also supports numerous joysticks and controllers. When you first run EmulationStation and it detects a game controller, it will launch a setup screen. This will allow you to configure your controller for the menu.

After your controller is configured, you will be at the menu screen, where you can select your system and game to be played.

When you first get to the menu, you will notice that it has few options available. This is because EmulationStation does not display emulators that do not have any game files available. Once you copy a ROM over, the system will appear.

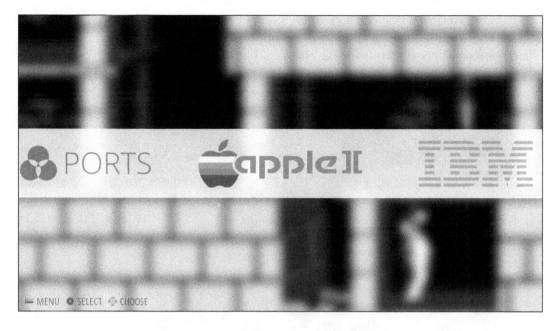

To setup your controller for the game systems, you will need to exit back out to the terminal. Then complete the following steps:

1. Run **sudo chown pi /opt/retropie/configs/all/retroarch.cfg**.

2. Then, run **cd /opt/retropie/emulators/RetroArch/installdir/ bin**.

3. Finally, run **sudo ./retroarch-joyconfig -j 0 >> /opt/ retropie/configs/all/retroarch.cfg**.

4. You will then be prompted to press your controller buttons.

5. When this is complete, run **sudo reboot** to reboot your Raspberry Pi.

Your controller will now be configured.

RetroPie has two ways to copy game files onto the Pi. The first is using SAMBA shares. These are essentially folders shared over your network. The following steps will explain how to use SAMBA shares to copy game files onto the Pi:

1. On Windows, you can access the folders by going to the network tab, or by entering the IP address of your Pi into the folder menu starting with two backslashes, for example, \\192.168.0.63.

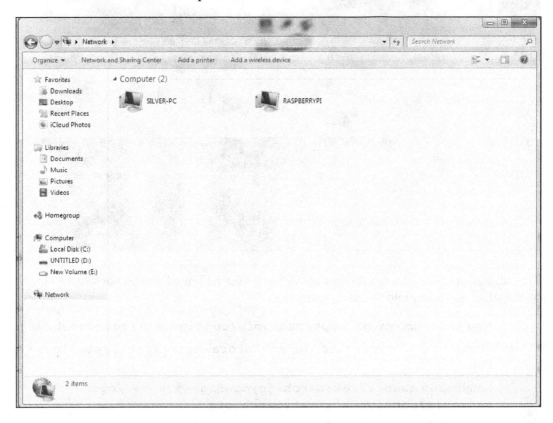

2. Double-click on `roms`, then on the system you wish to copy games to.

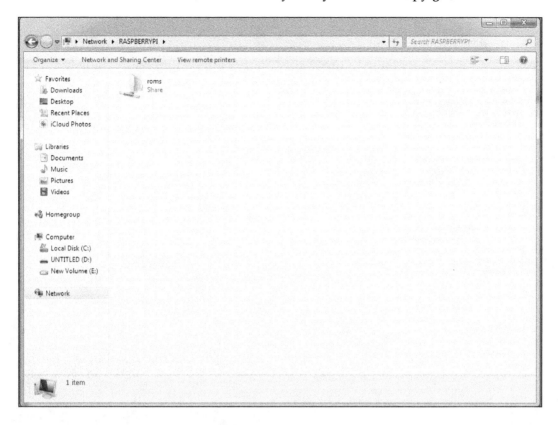

3. To copy your game files, drag and drop your game files into the folder.

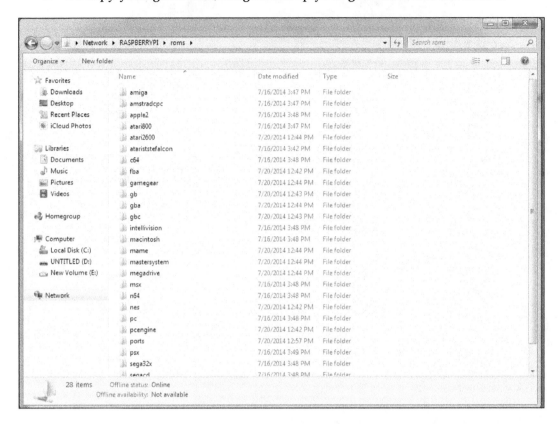

4. On OS X, select **Go**, select **Connect to Server**, and enter the server's IP address, for example, smb://192.168.0.63.

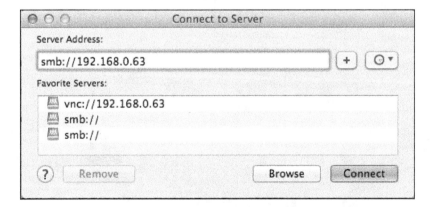

5. After clicking on **Connect**, you will be asked to log in as **Registered User** or as **Guest**. Choose **Guest**.

6. Then, click on **Connect** again and double-click on the `roms` menu choice. The `roms` folder is now shared to your computer. You will now have access to all the game file folders for RetroPie:

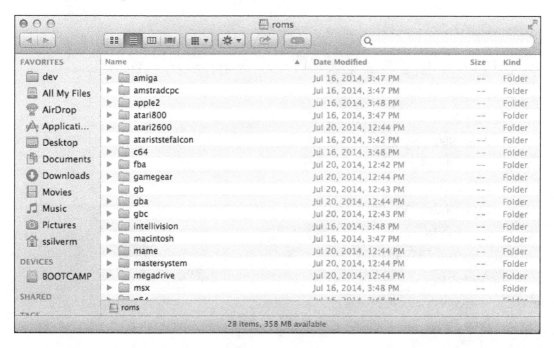

7. Now, simply drag and drop your game files to the proper folder, and get ready to play!

The second way is via USB drive. RetroPie keeps a service running in the background that detects when a new USB drive is inserted. The service checks for `roms` and game files on the drive via folders matching the system names. The service will automatically create the blank folders the first time you insert your USB drive. Just copy your files to the correct folder, and they will be moved to your SD card.

ChameleonPi

ChameleonPi is another ready-to-use Raspberry Pi distribution that focuses on the emulation of older computers. The ChameleonPi project was originally conceived to bring older and retro style computers to the Raspberry Pi device. To download ChameleonPi visit:

`http://chameleon.enging.com/`

ChameleonPi includes the following systems:

- ZX Spectrum
- Commodore 64
- Oric-1
- Oric Atmos
- Apple II series
- ZX81
- IBM PC
- Atari 800
- Atari 800XL
- Atari 2600
- Commodore Vic-20
- Commodore 128
- Amstrad CPC 464
- Atari ST
- Gameboy
- NES
- SNES
- Megadrive/Genesis

After booting up your Raspberry Pi with the ChameleonPi image, you should see the following splash screen:

After loading, the ChameleonPi the main menu will be displayed:

ChameleonPi offers a similar way to get game files onto the SD card as RetroPie does. The first is via SAMBA shares. The big difference between the two is that ChameleonPi's password protects the folders. By default, the username is zx and the password is spectrum. Once logged in, you will see a list of folders representing each system.

The other way is via the USB drive. Unlike RetroPie, where the files are copied from the USB drive to the SD card, ChameleonPi uses your USB drive as external storage. If you insert a freshly formatted drive, ChameleonPi will create a folder structure for your games. Copy your files into the corresponding folder on your USB drive, and then insert it into the Raspberry Pi. The next time you use ChameleonPi, your game files will appear.

Summary

In this chapter, you have been introduced to three different game-based Raspberry Pi distributions. While all three share a lot in common, they go about implementing gaming in their own unique ways. Try all three, and use the one that fits your gaming style the best.

In the next chapter, you will learn how to access the Raspberry Pi App Store so we can play with even more games.

4
Emulators

In this chapter, we will dive into emulation on the Raspberry Pi. But what is emulation? **Emulation** is the act of duplicating the functionality of one system onto another. This means that we can make the Raspberry Pi pretend to be something else, such as a Super Nintendo, or a Commodore 64, or a Sega Genesis. By utilizing different emulation software, our Raspberry Pi can be all these things and more.

You will learn:

- How to install applications using the Raspberry Pi App Store
- How to download applications from the Internet
- How to install programs from the Raspbian repositories

Let's start with the Raspberry Pi App Store.

Raspberry Pi App Store

It seems that a growing trend is for each device to have its own little ecosystem for applications. The Raspberry Pi is no different, and each copy of Raspbian has access to the Pi Store. This App Store is for you to download games and applications made specifically for the Raspberry Pi.

Using the App Store

We will now launch the App Store, create an account, and download some applications using the following steps:

1. At the command line, enter startx to start the desktop environment.
2. On the desktop, double-click on the Pi Store icon.

3. Click on the **Log In** link in the top-right corner of the window.

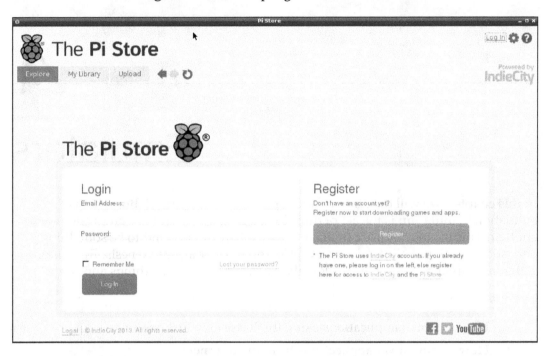

4. If you don't have an account yet, create one now, and then log in with the email address and password you used to register.

5. You can search for software using the search bar or click on a category to bring up applications and games specific to that area.

6. Click on the **Free Download** and/or **Buy Now** button when you have found a selection you would like to add to your library.

7. The selected item will be downloaded and automatically installed.

8. In the **My Library** tab, click on the item you want to run, and then click on the **Launch** button.

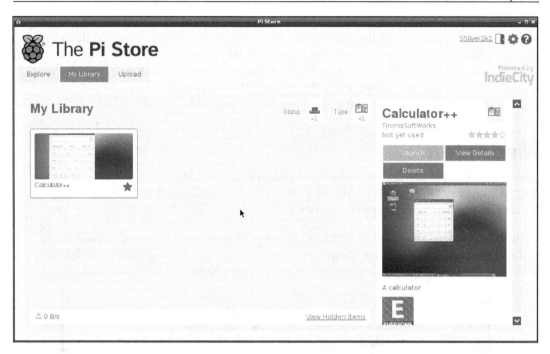

Any developer can sign up and upload their games to the store. Pricing for games starts at free of charge and can go up from there. Once the game has been made available in the store, any user with an account can purchase it. All games and apps are stored under the /usr/local/bin/indiecity folder to play them offline.

Don't worry about formatting your SD card and losing your games. When you log in to your Pi Store account you can re-download all your purchases.

Emulators

There are numerous emulators available for the Raspberry Pi. Some of these are available through the App Store, others you need to download from a website and manually install, and then there are some which can be installed via Raspbian's package manager.

Emulators recreate how a game console works, but they don't emulate the games themselves. That requires the game data. When we refer to game files in this book, we are referring to the **Read-Only Memory (ROM)** that a video game's data is stored on. These can be cartridges, CDs and DVDs, floppy disks, and other types of media. Many are available as files you can download. Please be aware that copyright may still exist on these files and that not all are freely available.

Mednafen

Mednafen is a program that consists of multiple system emulators. It can emulate the Atari Lynx, Neo Geo Pocket Color, WonderSwan, Game Boy Color, and the TurboGrafx-16 with great performance.

Installing Mednafen from the terminal is easy. We will use apt-get, which is the default package manager for Raspbian. The apt-get command makes it easy to install and update common Linux utilities and programs.

 Before using apt-get to install an application, you should run **sudo apt-get update**. This will keep the list of available applications up to date.

Let's see how to use the apt-get command:

1. In the command prompt, type sudo apt-get install mednafen and press *Enter*.

2. The apt-get command will now search the repositories for the application, download the package, and install it on your system. When it is completed, type mednafen and press *Enter*. You will be greeted with text that explains how to use the program.

3. This version is best run under the desktop, so type startx in the command prompt, and press *Enter*.

4. You will want to bring up the terminal app by double-clicking on **LXTerminal** from the desktop. You will also need to supply a game file to test with.

5. From the terminal, type mednafen /path/to/gamename and press *Enter*, for example, mednafen /home/pi/homebrew.zip.

6. Mednafen will read the game file, select the correct system, and bring up the game window.

You are now ready to play games using Mednafen.

FCEUX (NES)

FCEUX is an emulator designed to run games for the **Nintendo Entertainment System (NES)**. The NES is arguably the most popular and well known gaming system in video game history. Released in 1984, the NES introduced such popular titles as Super Mario Bros, The Legend of Zelda, MegaMan, and Metroid. Hundreds of games were produced for this 8-bit system, many of which can be played on the Raspberry Pi. The following steps will show you how to use FCEUX for running the game:

1. We will start by downloading FCEUX. Type `wget http://raspberrypigaming.com/files/fceux.zip` into your terminal.

2. Next, type `unzip fceux.zip` and press *Enter*. If you get the error saying unzip not found, type `sudo apt-get -y install unzip` to install the unzip program.

3. The file `fceux` should now be in your directory. Run the emulator by typing `./fceux /path/to/game/rom`, for example, `./fceux /home/pi/smb.nes`.

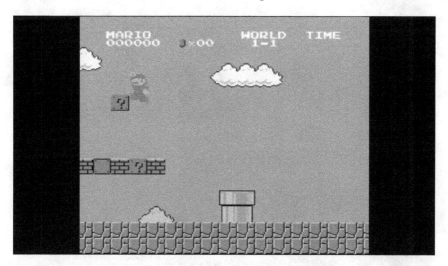

PiSNES (SNES)

PiSNES is a port of the SNES9x project and is an emulator designed to run games for the **Super Nintendo Entertainment System (SNES)**. The SNES was released in 1991, and featured 16-bit graphics, which was incredible for its time. The games released on the SNES are still highly sought after; collectors and players all around the world still enjoy games such as Final Fantasy, Star Fox, MegaMan X, F-Zero, Super Mario World, and hundreds of other great games. What makes this emulation possible, is the fact that PiSNES takes advantage of the Raspberry Pi's graphics chip, and offloads much of the processing to that.

PiSNES is not available in the Pi Store or the repositories, so we must download it from the project home page. We will be using wget to download the project files as follows:

1. First, we will create a folder for PiSNES. Type mkdir pisnes in a terminal.

2. Now, enter into the pisnes directory with cd pisnes.

3. Now, type wget http://raspberrypigaming.com/files/pisnes.zip. If that doesn't work, go to https://code.google.com/p/pisnes/ for the latest download.

4. Unzip the file by running unzip pisnes.zip.

5. Place your game files in the roms directory.

6. Now, run PiSNES with ./snes9x.gui.

7. A menu will appear with your available games. Have fun!

MAME4ALL

MAME4ALL is a port of the MAME project for the Raspberry Pi. **MAME** stands for **Multiple Arcade Machine Emulator**, and as its name implies, it is capable of running a large number of arcade games.

MAME4ALL is not available in the Pi Store or the repositories, so we must download it from the project home page. We will be using `wget` to download the project files as follows:

1. First, we will create a folder for MAME4ALL. Type `mkdir mame4all` in a terminal.
2. Now, enter into the `mame4all` directory with `cd mame4all`.
3. Next, type `wget http://raspberrypigaming.com/files/mame4all_ pi.zip`. If that doesn't work, go to `https://code.google.com/p/ mame4all-pi/` for the latest download.
4. Unzip the file by running `unzip mame4all_pi.zip`.
5. Place your game files in the `roms` directory.
6. Now, run MAME4ALL by typing `./mame`.
7. A menu will appear with your available games. Have fun!

FinalBurn Alpha

FinalBurn Alpha is a project designed to emulate many arcade games, most notably those that run on the Neo Geo, Capcom CPS-1, and CPS-2 platforms.

FinalBurn Alpha is not available in the Pi Store or the repositories, so we must download it from the project home page. We will be using `wget` to download the project files.

1. First, we will create a folder for FinalBurn Alpha. Type `mkdir fba` in a terminal.

2. Now, enter into the `fba` directory with `cd fba`.

3. Next, type `wget http://raspberrypigaming.com/files/fba.zip`. If that doesn't work, go to `https://code.google.com/p/pifba/` for the latest download.

4. Unzip the file by running `unzip fba.zip`.

5. Place your game files in the `roms` directory.

6. Now, run FinalBurn Alpha with `./fbacapex`.

7. A menu will appear with your available games. Have fun!

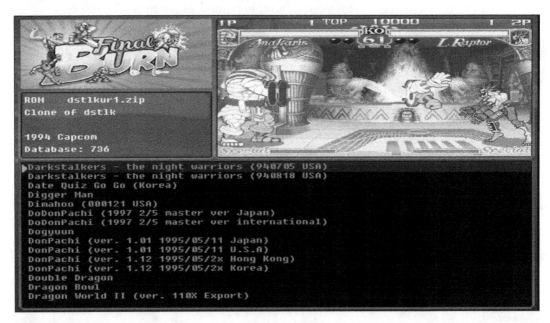

PCSX_ReARMed

PCSX_ReARMed is a PlayStation emulator for the Raspberry Pi. As crazy as this seems, the Raspberry Pi can play PlayStation games! The reason for this is that the Raspberry Pi has a very powerful graphics chip that runs OpenGL ES code. PCSX_ReARMed has been written to take advantage of OpenGL ES, which gives us a great emulator.

PCSX_ReARMed is available for free on the Pi Store. Make use of the following steps to download it:

1. Once you are on the desktop and logged into the Pi Store, click on the **Games** tab. You can also search for `PCSX_Rearmed`.

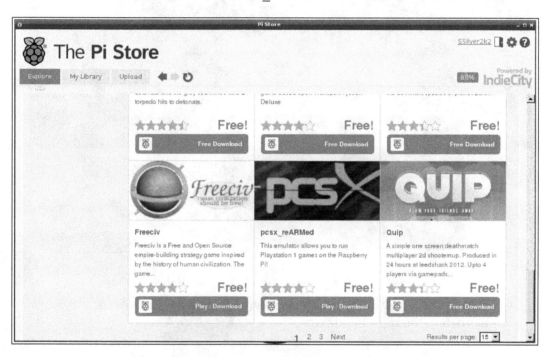

2. Click on **Play/Download** to begin the installation process.

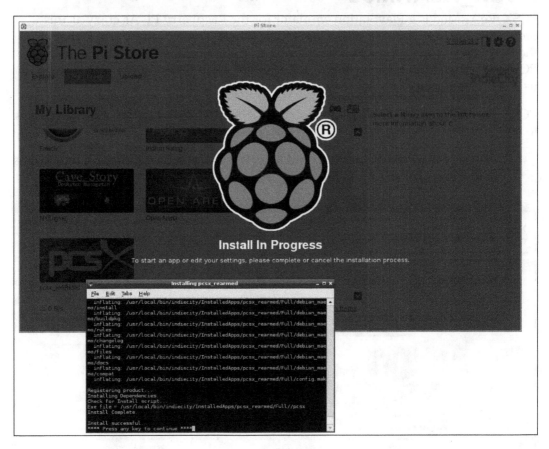

3. When instructed, press any key to finish the installation.
4. To run the program, go to **My Library**, click on **pcsx_reARMed**, and press **Launch** in the right-hand panel.

5. Click on **Execute** and the PCSX_ReARMed game window will appear.

6. You don't need to place your games in any specific directory for this emulator. When you select **Load CD image**, you can browse the Raspberry Pi's file system for your game file.

PicoDrive (Genesis/Mega Drive)

PicoDrive is an emulator that runs games made for the Sega Genesis (also known as the Mega Drive in Japan and Europe). The Genesis is a 16-bit gaming console that came out in 1989. It was known for its many great arcade ports, such as Altered Beast and Mortal Kombat, as well as a series that has spanned numerous releases and consoles, Sonic The Hedgehog. To download PicoDrive go through the following steps:

1. Type `wget http://raspberrypigaming.com/files/picodrive.tgz` in your terminal.

2. Next, type `tar zxfv picrodrive.tgz` and press *Enter*. A long list of files will stream across the screen.

3. You should now have a directory called `picodrive`. Enter the directory by typing `cd picodrive`.

4. Run the emulator by typing `./PicoDrive`. The PicoDrive menu should appear on your screen:

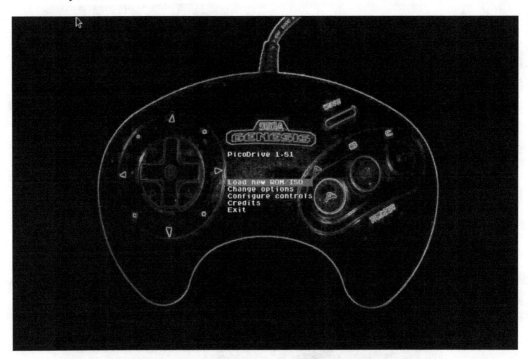

5. Use the menu option **Load new ROM/ISO**, which will traverse your Raspberry Pi's directories and select your ROM file to be played.

Stella (Atari 2600)

Now, for the granddaddy of all gaming systems, the Atari 2600. It was released in 1977 and ushered in the video game craze. For the first time, popular arcade games could be brought home, new properties could be created, and a whole new market opened up. From arcade ports such as Pac Man and Donkey Kong to the original games such as Pitfall, and even infamous games such as E.T., the Atari 2600 has a very rich history of gaming. Stella is an emulator that aims to bring this console to the Raspberry Pi using the following steps:

1. The installation is super simple; just type `sudo apt-get install stella` to install Stella on the console and press *Enter*.

2. After a few moments, `apt-get` should finish, and Stella will be installed.

3. To run Stella, just type `stella` and press *Enter*.

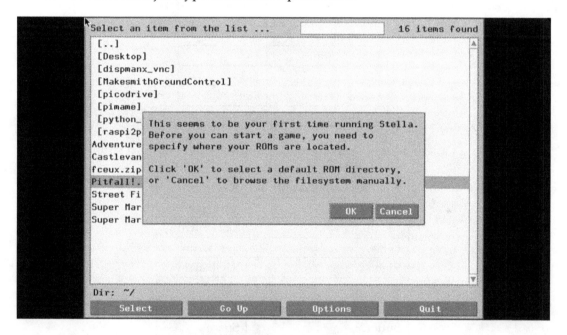

4. Use the arrows and *tab* keys to navigate your Pi for game files. Then, highlight the **Select** button and press *Enter*.

Controls

Now that you have installed some emulators, you will want to know how to control the games. Here is a cheat sheet for the default keys in PiSNES:

PiSNES controls	Keyboard
Up	Up arrow
Down	Down arrow
Left	Left arrow
Right	Right arrow
A	D
B	C
X	S
Y	X
Left Bumper	A
Right Bumper	F
Start	Enter
Select	Tab
To quit	Esc

The following table is a cheat sheet for the default keys in FinalBurn Alpha:

FinalBurn Alpha controls	Keyboard
Up	Up arrow
Down	Down arrow
Left	Left arrow
Right	Right arrow
Button 1	Ctrl
Button 2	Alt
Button 3	Space
Button 4	Shift
Button 5	Z
Button 6	X
Start	Enter
Coin	Tab
To quit	Esc

Because PiSNES and FinalBurn Alpha were ported to the Raspberry Pi by the same person, they share similar configuration files. Within their respective directories, you will find a configuration file that allows you to change the control scheme. PiSNES is called `snes9x.cfg`, and FinalBurn Alpha is called `fba2x.cfg`. The keyboard section uses numbers to represent each key. You can find them by reading the output of `/usr/include/SDL/SDL_keysym.h`.

The following table is a cheat sheet for the default keys in MAME4ALL:

MAME4ALL Controls	Keyboard
Up	Up arrow
Down	Down arrow
Left	Left arrow
Right	Right arrow
Button 1	*Ctrl*
Button 2	*Alt*
Button 3	Space
Button 4	*Shift*
Button 5	Z
Button 6	X
Start	*1*
Coin	*5*
To quit	*Esc*

To change the controls in MAME4ALL, press the *Tab* key to bring up the configuration menu. This will allow you to globally map the controls to your gamepad, keyboard, joystick, or individual games.

The PCSX_ReARMed controls can be seen and edited within the controls on the main screen.

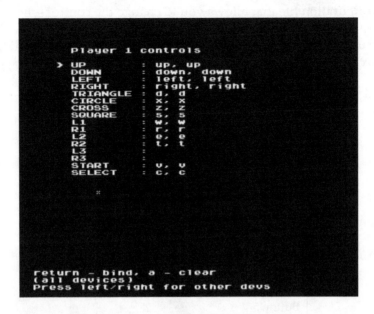

PicoDrive controls can be edited from within the main menu.

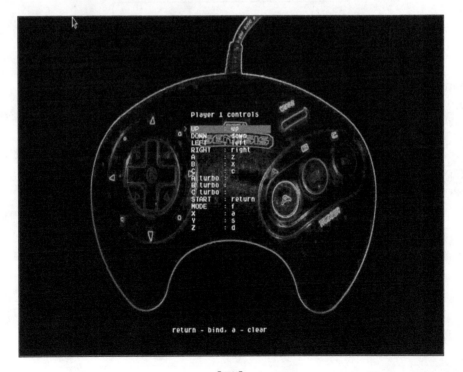

The following table is a cheat sheet for the default keys in Stella:

Stella	Keyboard
Up	Up arrow
Down	Down arrow
Left	Left arrow
Right	Right arrow
Reset	F2
Select game type	F1
Fire/Action	Space or *Ctrl*
Select game	*Enter*
To quit	*Esc*

To edit Stella's controls, highlight and select *Options*, and then click on **Input Settings**.

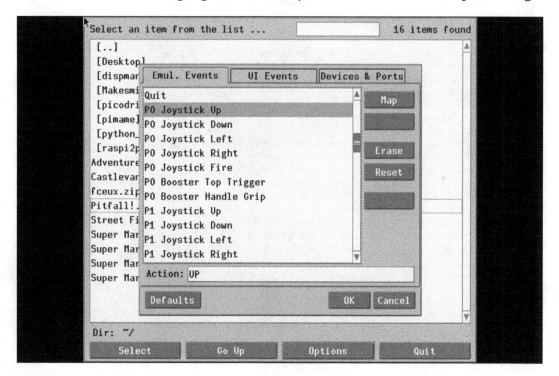

Summary

You learned how easy it is to use the Raspberry Pi's *Pi Store* application, which is included in every copy of Raspbian. From setting up your account, to purchasing new games, the Pi Store is a great resource. You also installed some emulators on your Pi using the various installation methods available in Linux, and played some classic video games.

In the next chapter, we will introduce standalone games that have been ported over to the Raspberry Pi.

5
Ported Games

Now that we have played some games via an emulator, we are ready to play some games that were ported to work on the Raspberry Pi. A port is a piece of software that is coded and developed for a specific environment but has been transported and rebuilt for a different one. This commonly occurs with console games. A game will be written for a Microsoft console, and then ported over to Sony's or Nintendo's console. It also happens when a console game is ported over to the PC.

This chapter will focus on those games that have been released for other platforms, and then ported over to the Raspberry Pi.

You will learn how to:

- Install and play Cave Story
- Install and play Doom
- Install and play Open Arena, and create a multiplayer server for it
- Install, create your own world, and program scripts for Minecraft

Cave Story

Cave Story is a freeware Metroid/Castlevania style platformer. It is a massive platform adventure along the lines of Metroid, Castlevania, and Terraria. With a long engrossing storyline, a hard but not frustrating difficulty level, and a beautiful setting, the game is perfect to sit back and lose a few hours with. It was originally released on the PC for Microsoft Windows in 2004. Over the years, it has been ported to the Nintendo Wii, DSi, 3DS, Mac OS X, and Linux.

The Raspberry Pi port is possible because the original Cave Story engine was reverse engineered and a new open source engine called NXEngine was created.

Installing and running

Installing Cave Story is very simple. It can be done by performing the following steps:

1. First, we need to download Cave Story. At the command line, type `wget http://raspberrypigaming.com/files/cavestory.zip`. You can also find the source code at `http://nxengine.sourceforge.net/` and `https://github.com/ssilverm/cavestory_rpi`.

2. Next, run `unzip cavestory.zip`. The files will be extracted to a folder called `cavestory_rpi-master`.

3. Enter the directory by typing `cd cavestory_rpi-master`.

4. Now, let's run Cave Story by typing `./nx`.

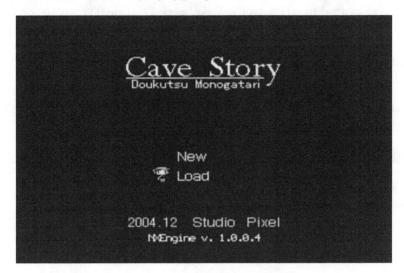

Controls

Here is a list of the default keys in Cave Story:

Action	Key
Left	Left arrow
Right	Right arrow
Up	Up arrow

Action	Key
Down	Down arrow
Jump	Z
Fire	X
Prev weapon	A
Next weapon	S
Inventory	Q
Map	W
Quit	Esc
Options	F3

Doom

When you think of a **first-person shooter** (**FPS**), modern games like Call of Duty or Halo might come to mind, but before these was Doom. The great grandfather of the modern FPS, Doom, created by id Software, took the PC gaming world by storm. For its time, Doom had amazing graphics, multiplayer capabilities, user-created levels, and introduced the concept of shareware. It included the first chapter of the game for free, but if you wanted to finish the story and beat the game, you were asked to purchase the game. Doom made history. When id Software open sourced the Doom engine, players and developers quickly scoured the code. They made updates, patched bugs, added new features, and most importantly, ported the game to multiple systems.

Doom is still being developed today. If we take advantage of modern capabilities and modern 3D graphics cards, the original game can be made to look better. For Raspberry Pi, we will go for the classic style.

PrBoom is a Linux port of the Doom engine that includes the Freedoom campaign. Freedoom is a totally new set of levels to play in the Doom universe.

Installing and running

We will install PrBoom using `apt-get`, as follows:

1. At the command line, type `sudo apt-get install prboom`.

2. Press **Y** when it asks to install.

3. Now, let's run PrBoom by typing `prboom` and pressing *Enter*.

4. You are going to be presented with the Freedoom campaign. Press *Enter* to begin and then choose your difficulty level.

The awesome Doom community has created hundreds of campaigns. They are stored in files called WADs. If you want to change the campaign, download some WAD files to your Raspberry Pi and run PrBoom with the command `prboom -file /path/to/game.wad`.

Controls

Here is a list of the default keys in Doom:

Action	Key
Turn left	Left arrow
Turn right	Right arrow
Forward	Up arrow
Back	Down arrow

Action	Key
Action	Space
Fire	*Ctrl*
Change weapon	Press 2 through 7
Menu	*Esc*

Open Arena

What PrBoom is to Doom, Open Arena is to Quake 3 Arena. Quake 3 Arena is another innovator of the FPS genre. It helped launch a hugely competitive multiplayer environment as well as a race for a better graphics card to churn out more frames per second. The Quake 3 engine has been used for a staggering number of games. Since id Software open sourced the engine, it is capable of running on the Raspberry Pi. Open Arena is a project to develop a completely free version of Quake 3 Arena. Using entirely new sprites, 3D models, textures, and levels, anyone can download Open Arena to their computer and play for free.

Installation

Open Arena is available on the Raspberry Pi App Store. Make use of the following steps to install Open Arena:

1. From the command line, enter startx to launch the desktop environment.

2. From the desktop, launch the Pi Store application by double-clicking on the Pi Store icon.

3. At the top-right of the application, there will be a login link. Click the link and log in with your registered account.

4. Navigate to **Explore | Games | Fighting**.

5. Click on the **Open Arena** result.

6. At the application info page, click on the **Play/Download** button on the right-hand side of the screen.

7. Open Arena will automatically be downloaded and a window will appear showing the installation progress.

8. Press any button to close the window once it has finished installing.

9. When you click on **Launch** to play the game, your Raspberry Pi will reboot and automatically launch Open Arena on the command line.

Single player match

For a single player campaign, perform the following steps:

1. From the Open Arena main menu, click on **SINGLE PLAYER**.

2. Select one of the map icons from the list. The opponents in the arena will be listed at the bottom.

3. Click on **fight** to load the arena and start the match.

Multiplayer match

FPS are fun on their own with bots, but to really enjoy the full experience, you need to play with other people. Sadly, the Raspberry Pi version is not compatible with the PC servers, so most of the multiplayer games you see online will not work. The good news is that you can create your own server!

Running a server

To start your own server, perform the following actions:

1. From the command line, change into the Open Arena directory by typing `cd /usr/local/bin/indiecity/InstalledApps/openarena/Full/`.
2. Execute the `oadedicated` script by running `./oadedicated.sh`.
3. After `Opening IP Socket` appears, press *Enter*.
4. In the command prompt, type `map oa_dm3` and press *Enter*.
5. The Open Arena dedicated server will now be running on your local network.
6. Other Pi using Open Arena can now connect to your Raspberry Pi's IP address.

Joining a server

To join a server created by another user, perform the following actions:

1. From the Open Arena main menu, click on **MULTI PLAYER**.
2. Edit your player name and customize your character as required.
3. Click on **next**.
4. Open Arena will search for servers on your local network.
5. If your local game does not appear, click on **specify** and enter the IP address of the server you wish to join. If the server is running on the same Pi you wish to play on, you can enter `127.0.0.1` (This is called a loopback address. It means connecting to itself).

Controls

The following is a list of the default keys in Open Arena:

Action	Key
Strafe left	*A*
Strafe right	*D*
Forward	*W*
Back	*S*
Jump	Space
Fire	Left mouse click
Change weapon	Press *1* through *9* or use your mouse wheel
Menu	*Esc*
Aim	Mouse click

Minecraft: Pi Edition

Minecraft is a sandbox-style game made by the game company Mojang. Because it is a sandbox, there is no right or wrong way to play it. The concept behind the game is that you explore and build using different kinds of blocks in a randomly created world. It has been compared to a virtual LEGO set. If you can think it, you can build it in Minecraft.

It was originally developed for the Windows PC, but has since been ported to OS X, iOS, Android, and various game consoles. Mojang developed and released a port to the Raspberry Pi as a free download.

Installing and running

If you are running the latest version of Raspbian, Minecraft is now included by default. If you are running an older version of Raspbian, you can install Minecraft using apt-get, as follows:

1. At the command line, type sudo apt-get update.

2. Then, type sudo apt-get install minecraft-pi.

3. From the desktop, double-click on the Minecraft Pi Edition icon, or from a desktop terminal, type minecraft-pi and press *Enter*.

Creating a new Minecraft world

To create a new Minecraft world, perform the following actions:

1. With Minecraft running, click on **Start Game**.

2. Select **Create new**.

3. After a few moments, you will enter into a brand new Minecraft world environment.

Using the Minecraft: Pi Edition Application Programming Interface

Now that you have created your Minecraft world, you can explore, fight creepers, create your own castle, and whatever else your mind can think of. The Raspberry Pi Edition includes something extra—a programming interface. You can use the Python programming language to hook into Minecraft and edit the game world with lines of code.

To use the Minecraft API, perform the following actions:

1. Start the Python interactive shell by running `python` on the terminal.

2. You will see >>>, which is where you will enter the Python commands.

3. Enter the following commands:
   ```
   from mcpi import minecraft
   from mcpi import block
   mc = minecraft.Minecraft.create()
   mc.postToChat("I am using the API!")
   ```

4. You should now see `I am using the API` message appear in your Minecraft window.

5. Enter the following commands:
   ```
   player = mc.player.getPos()
   player
   ```

6. An output similar to `Vec3(46.0,1.0,-14.0)` should appear.

7. Enter the next command:
   ```
   mc.setBlock(player.x +1, player.y, player.z, block.GOLD_BLOCK)
   ```

8. A golden block should appear directly in front of you:

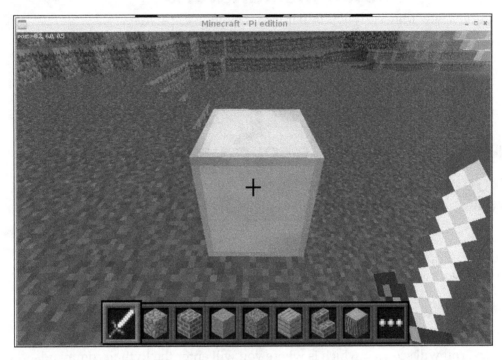

There are many more things you can do with both Python and the Minecraft API. From creating functions that will build a fortress to using loops to stack tons of TNT blocks, you can program the entire world.

For more API documentation, visit:

`http://www.stuffaboutcode.com/p/minecraft-api-reference.html`

Multiplayer Minecraft

Minecraft: Pi Edition is a multiplayer game. If you have other people running Raspberry Pis on your network, all they need to do is click on **Join Game** in the main menu, and all the currently running Minecraft worlds will be available for them to join.

Controls

Here is a list of the default keys in Minecraft:

Action	Key
Forward	*W*
Left	*A*
Down	*S*
Right	*D*
Inventory	*E*
Jump	Space
Fly/Fall	Double space
Menu	*Esc*
Place block	Left mouse click
Remove block	Right mouse click
Select quick inventory	*1 – 9* or mouse wheel

Summary

In this chapter, you learned how to download and install some games, which were remade for the Raspberry Pi. You learned how to install games via `apt-get` like PrBoom, download games from the Internet like Cave Story, set up a multiplayer server for Open Arena, and program your own Minecraft world.

In the next chapter, we will discuss games made just for Linux and the Raspberry Pi.

6
Linux Games

So far, we have gone over emulation and ported games. What we haven't talked about yet, is games that were made with Linux in mind. These are games that were designed for, and native to, the Linux operating system. Usually free and open source, they are games that have communities built around them, and welcome others to submit code back into the game.

This chapter will focus on a few of those free open source games available in the Raspbian repository.

In this chapter, you will learn:

- How to install, run, and setup a network server for FreeCiv
- How to install and play SuperTux, a Super Mario Bros. clone
- How to install and play Njam, a Pac-Man clone
- How to install and play Galaga: Hyperspace, a Galaga/Galaxian clone

FreeCiv

FreeCiv is a free, open source, turn-based strategy game that is influenced by the long running civilization series of games. In FreeCiv, you take on the role leading your chosen civilization out of the Stone Age and into the Space Age. You must explore, build out, and research new skills and abilities, all while trying to defeat the rival civilizations that are doing the same thing. FreeCiv has been in development for over 18 years and boasts a large community with years of information and resources.

FreeCiv features various difficulties of AI, single player and multiplayer capabilities, randomly generated maps, rule fine-tuning, and tons of other things to make each game a totally different experience.

Installing and running

Installing FreeCiv is very simple. Follow these steps:

1. At the command line, type `sudo apt-get install -y freeciv-client-gtk`. This will install FreeCiv, as well as the FreeCiv server.

2. Once the install is finished, make sure you are on the desktop environment by typing `startx` and pressing *Enter*.

3. Once you are on the desktop, click on the menu button at the bottom-left and highlight **Games**. Under the sub menu, you will see the **Freeciv** option. Click on it.

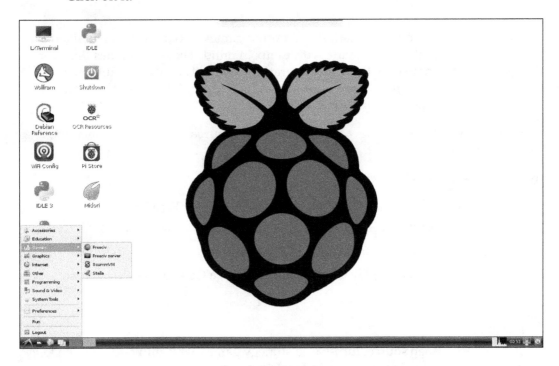

4. FreeCiv should now have launched and you will be presented with a few options.

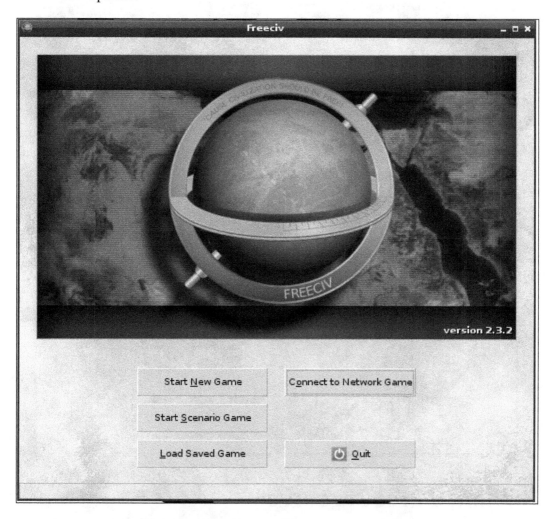

5. Select **Start New Game** and you will be presented with the game setup screen. Here, you will able to set the game options, choose the amount of players, and pick which nation you will be playing as.

6. Click on **Start** to begin the game.

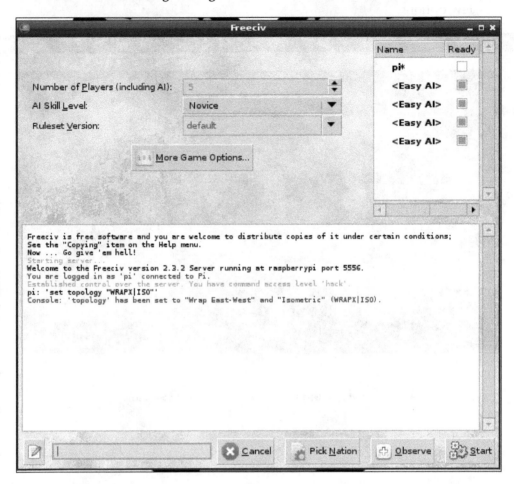

Hosting a FreeCiv server

Playing FreeCiv against the AI is a great way to learn and get good at the game, but the game really shines when you include your friends (or soon to be enemies).

The Raspberry Pi serves as a great platform to host a multiplayer FreeCiv game. Just use the following steps:

1. From the desktop menu, select **Games** and then click on **Freeciv server**. A command window will open and automatically start a new game.

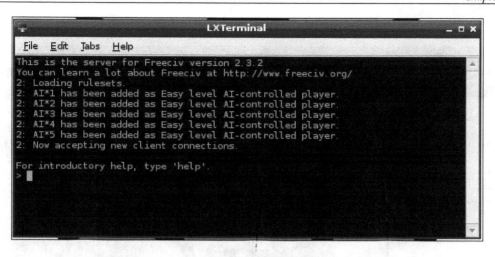

2. Now, load FreeCiv, and click on **Connect to Network Game**. Your game server should appear in the list of available games.

3. Double-click on the desired game to join it.

4. When you are ready, click on **Start** and the game will begin! Good Luck!

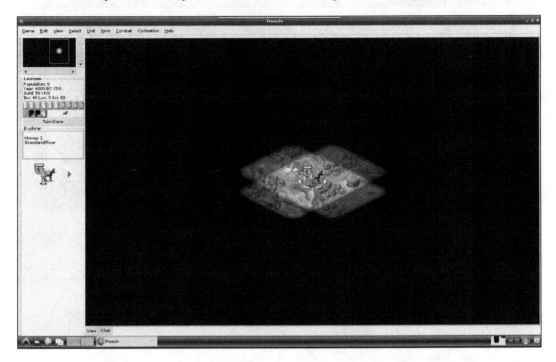

Learning the controls

FreeCiv is a complicated game, as you can see from the control list below. Your mouse and menu options will usually be enough; so don't get discouraged by the sheer amount of options. Most of these you won't need until you get through a few games. These controls were retrieved from the official FreeCiv website:

`http://freeciv.wikia.com/wiki/Keyboard_Reference`

Reports	
Cities	*F4*
Demographics	*F11*
Economy	*F5*
Map view	*F1*
Messages	*F9*
Nations	*F3*
Research	*F6*
Spaceship	*F12*

Top Five Cities	*F8*
Units	*F2*
Wonders of the World	*F7*
General	
Close Dialog / Abort	*Esc*
Edit Worklists	*Ctrl + l*
Editor Mode	*Ctrl + e*
Find City	*Ctrl + f*
Game menu	*F10*
Quit Game	*Ctrl + q*
Revolution	*Shift + Ctrl + r*
Save Game	*Ctrl + s*
Tax Rates	*Ctrl + t*
Toggle Fog of war (in Editor Mode)	*Ctrl + m*
Turn Done	*Shift* + return
Unit commands	
Auto Explore	*x*
Auto Settler	*a*
Build Airport	*e*
Build City	*b*
Build Fortress	*F*
Build Irrigation	*i*
Build Mine	*m*
Build Roads/ Rails	*r*
Change Forest to Plains	*i*
Change Forest to Swamp	*m*
Change Jungle to Forest	*m*
Change Jungle to Grassland	*i*

Clean Nuclear Fallout	*n*
Clean Pollution	*p*
Connect Rail/Road	*R*
Connect Irrigation	*I*
Diplomat/Spy Actions	*d*
Disband Unit	*D*
Done	*Space*
Explode Nuke	*N*
Fortify unit(s)	*f*
Go to	*g*
Go to Build City	*B*
Go/Airlift to City	*t*
Load Transporter	*l*
Make Homecity	*h*
Patrol	*q*
Return to nearest City	*G*
Select Units of the same type	*v*
Select Units of the same type on the same tile	*V*
Sentry Unit(s)	*s*
Transform Terrain	*o*
Unload	*u*
Unload Transporter	*T*
Upgrade Unit	*U*

Wait	w
Wake up others	*Shift + w*
View commands	
Center View on Unit	*c*
City Growth	*Ctrl + r*
City Names	*Ctrl + n*
City Outlines	*Ctrl + y*
City Production	*Ctrl + p*
City Trade routes	*Ctrl + d*
City Worker Output	*Ctrl + w*
Full Screen Mode	*Alt + Enter*
Map Grid	*Ctrl + g*
National Borders	*Ctrl + b*

SuperTux

SuperTux is another free and open source Linux game. Being reminiscent of the Super Mario Bros. series, it is a side-scrolling action game, where the goal of the game is to rescue Penny by getting from one end of the level to the other, while killing or avoiding enemies, and collecting power-ups. SuperTux includes 26 levels, but there is also a level editor available, so you can make your own stages.

Installing and running

SuperTux is included in the Raspbian software repositories, and can be played on the terminal or desktop environment using the following steps:

1. At the command line, type `sudo apt-get install -y supertux`.

2. To run the game, type `supertux` and press *Enter*. The game should now fill your entire screen.

3. Use the up and down arrow keys to select **Start Game**, then press *Enter* to begin playing SuperTux.

Learning the controls

Here is a list of the keys that you would require in the game:

Action	Keyboard
Left	Left arrow
Right	Right arrow
Activate/Enter	Up arrow
Duck	Down arrow
Jump	Space
Use ability	Left control
Menu	*Esc*

Njam

Njam is also a free open source game based on classic maze games like Pac-Man. The goal of the game is to eat all the dots while avoiding the obstacles. If you eat one of the power-ups, you gain invincibility for a short period of time. Njam includes an array of levels, level editors, and multiplayer capabilities.

Installing and running

Njam is available in the Raspbian software repositories, and can be played on the terminal or desktop environment using the following steps:

1. At the command line, type `sudo apt-get install -y njam`.

2. To run the game, type `njam` and press *Enter*. The game should now fill your entire screen.

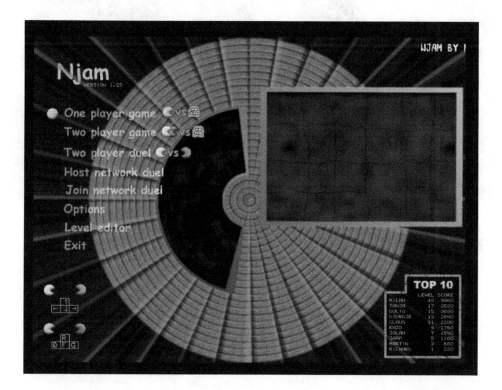

3. Njam offers a single-player game, two-player cooperative mode, two-player duel mode, and a 4-player network game. To play a local game, just select **One player game** or **Two player game**. You will then select a map and start playing.

4. Playing a network game is easy as well. If you are hosting the game, just select **Host network duel**. The other players will need to select **Join network duel** from their copies of Njam, and enter in your IP address. Once everyone has readied up, press the spacebar to start the game.

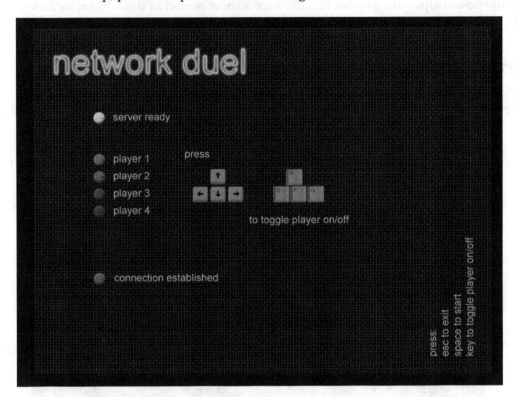

Learning the controls

Here is a list of keys that you would require in the game:

Action	Keyboard
Up	Up arrow
Down	Down arrow
Left	Left arrow
Right	Right arrow
Exit	*Esc*

Galaga: Hyperspace

Galaga: Hyperspace is a game based on classic shoot 'em up games like Galaga and Galaxian. The goal of the game is to destroy each wave of aliens while avoiding the bullets they hurl your way. Each wave gets more and more difficult, and you can only get hit once before losing a life.

Installing and running

Galaga: Hyperspace is available in the Raspbian software repositories, and can only be played on the desktop environment using the following steps:

1. At the command line, type `sudo apt-get install -y xgalaga`.
2. To run the game, make sure you are on the desktop environment by typing `startx` and then pressing *Enter*.
3. Once you are on the desktop, click on the menu button at the bottom-left and highlight **Games**. Under the sub menu, **Galaga** will be an option. Click on it to start the game.

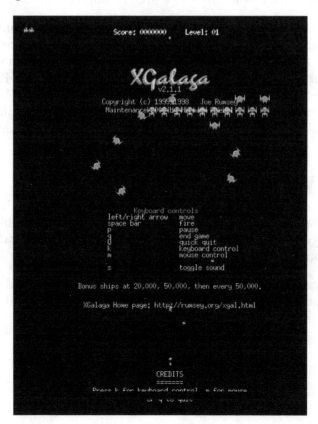

Learning the controls

Here is a list of the keys that you would require in the game:

Action	Keyboard
Left	Left arrow
Right	Right arrow
Start Game with keyboard controls	K
Start Game with mouse controls	M
Quit Galaga: Hyperspace	Q
Quit current game	q

Finding games via the repositories

The games mentioned above are just the tip of the iceberg when it comes to Linux gaming. The Raspbian repositories include a ton of packages, and there are a few commands you should know in order to search through it.

The `apt-cache search keyword` command will search the repos for the keyword you specify, and display a list of results in the command terminal. For example: `apt-cache search game` will display pages of results. You can then whittle down the results by specifying multiple keywords. Let's say we want to find a Pac-Man clone: `apt-cache search pacman` will return a list of games that include Pac-Man in the description. The `apt-cache search pacman console` command will further refine the search and will return one result that matches your query, `pacman4console`.

Summary

In this chapter, you learned about games that were made specifically for Linux and that run on Raspberry Pi. There are dozens more games available in the repositories that you can install and try out. From roguelikes to arcade remakes, the repos hold hours of fun.

In the next chapter, we will discuss the various input methods available for the Raspberry Pi, including arcade sticks, Bluetooth controllers, and gaming console devices.

7
Controllers

In this chapter, we will go through many of the types of gaming input devices that we can connect to our Raspberry Pi. From fightsticks (or joysticks), gamepads, console controllers, to building your own, there are all sorts of options available.

In this chapter, you will learn how to:

- Enable Bluetooth connectivity
- Set up Xbox and PlayStation controllers
- Use a USB encoder
- Use the GPIO pins to build your own controller
- Troubleshoot problem controllers

Controllers on the Raspberry Pi

Before we begin, you will want to install the joystick package to your device. Type sudo apt-get -y install joystick at the command line and press *Enter*. The joystick package includes an application called jstest, which will help you identify and troubleshoot your controllers.

When a controller is connected and recognized by the Raspberry Pi, a new entry will be made in the /dev/input/ folder. This folder contains a list of all connected input devices. You should see files like event0, mouse0, and kb0 depending on what has been connected. When your controller is connected, you should see a new item called js0. The 0 at the end of the item indicates the order in which it was connected. You can have multiple items connected, and they will each get an increasing number.

Gamepads

Gamepads are one of the simplest types of controllers for the Raspberry Pi. They can come in different shapes, sizes, and can have different combinations of buttons. These types of controllers are usually modeled after popular consoles, and made to look like NES, SNES, Genesis, or PlayStation gamepads. The major advantage of these is that they are compact, handheld, and very portable.

As long as the gamepad is connected via USB, it will be Plug and Play on the Raspberry Pi.

Arcade sticks

Arcade sticks, also known as fightsticks, are a very popular choice to connect to the Pi. Fightsticks come in hundreds of variations, and can be custom-built, custom-configured, upgraded, and modified. In all likelihood, you won't find two pro fightsticks that are 100 percent the same.

The reason behind this, is that each person has their own preference when it comes to buttons, joysticks, and encoders. Some people prefer the American style Happ buttons, while others swear by the Sanwa Japanese style buttons. There are those who prefer ball top joysticks while others use bat style joysticks.

The great part about this, is that the button sizes and joysticks are generally interchangeable. Buttons can be swapped around, and joysticks commonly use two different screw variations.

Just like gamepads, Arcade sticks connect easily to the USB port of a Raspberry Pi and should be just Plug and Play.

Xbox 360 controllers

Xbox 360 controllers come in two varieties: wired and wireless. Wired Xbox 360 controllers are Plug and Play in the latest version of Raspbian.

When you plug in your controller, the guide lights will blink on and off repeatedly. If you wish to have it function like an actual Xbox controller, where only the single-player guide light is activated, you will need to use a free open source program called **xboxdrv**. Xboxdrv allows you to customize buttons, activate a controller, and use the wireless USB adapter for Xbox 360 controllers. Follow the given steps to install xboxdrv:

1. Type `sudo apt-get -y install xboxdrv` on the command line and press *Enter*.

2. To test whether it works, plug in your Xbox controller, type `sudo xboxdrv --kernel-detach-driver` and press *Enter*.

3. The lights on the controller should stop blinking and be replaced with one solid light.

4. Pressing any button will cause your screen to list the current status of each button.

5. Press *Ctrl + C* to close xboxdrv.

```
pi@raspberrypi ~ $ sudo xboxdrv --detach-kernel-driver --silent &
[1] 2623
pi@raspberrypi ~ $ xboxdrv 0.8.4 - http://pingus.seul.org/~grumbel/xboxdrv/
Copyright © 2008-2011 Ingo Ruhnke <grumbel@gmx.de>
Licensed under GNU GPL version 3 or later <http://gnu.org/licenses/gpl.html>
This program comes with ABSOLUTELY NO WARRANTY.
This is free software, and you are welcome to redistribute it under certain conditions; see the file
COPYING for details.

Controller:         Microsoft Xbox 360 Controller
Vendor/Product:     045e:028e
USB Path:           001:010
Controller Type:    Xbox360

Your Xbox/Xbox360 controller should now be available as:
  /dev/input/js1
  /dev/input/event4

Press Ctrl-c to quit

pi@raspberrypi ~ $
```

To use xboxdrv normally, type `sudo xboxdrv --kernel-detach-driver --silent &` and press *Enter*. This will activate xboxdrv, suppress the screen output whenever a button is pressed, and launch it in the background, so you can still use your Pi for other things. Just run through the following steps:

1. To activate xboxdrv at login, type `nano ~/.profile`.

2. Use the arrow keys to go to the end of the file.

3. Type `sudo xboxdrv --kernel-detach-driver --silent &`.

4. Press *Ctrl + X* and then press *Y* to save the file.

5. Now, when you log in to your Pi, xboxdrv will automatically launch and set up your Xbox controller.

If you want to run multiple Xbox controllers on the same Pi, you will need to launch another instance of xboxdrv.

Sony DualShock 3 controllers

Sony DualShock 3 controllers are very neat. They can be connected to the Raspberry Pi via USB or Bluetooth, and have motion sensors that are read as different axes. The DualShock 3 is Plug and Play compatible with Raspbian, when using the USB cable.

Simply hook up a Micro USB cable end to the controller, and a standard USB cable end to the Pi and you will be ready to go. The Pi will also charge the controller's internal battery. If you are using more than one controller, or you experience odd behavior, switch to a powered USB hub.

Setting it up for Bluetooth connectivity requires that you perform the following steps:

1. First, ensure that you have a Raspberry Pi compatible Bluetooth dongle. Most inexpensive dongles will work, but a list of working products is available at `http://elinux.org/RPi_USB_Bluetooth_adapters`.

2. Type `sudo apt-get -y install bluez-utils bluez-compat bluez-hcidump libusb-dev libbluetooth-dev`. This install will take a few minutes.

3. After the install is finished, type `hciconfig` and make sure your Bluetooth dongle is listed.

```
pi@raspberrypi ~ $ hciconfig
hci0:   Type: BR/EDR  Bus: USB
        BD Address: 00:02:5B:00:A5:A5   ACL MTU: 310:10   SCO MTU: 64:8
        UP RUNNING PSCAN
        RX bytes:1483 acl:0 sco:0 events:72 errors:0
        TX bytes:1334 acl:0 sco:0 commands:71 errors:0

pi@raspberrypi ~ $
```

4. Now, you will need to download, compile, and install sixad. Download sixad by typing `wget http://sourceforge.net/projects/qtsixa/files/QtSixA%201.5.1/QtSixA-1.5.1-src.tar.gz`. If the page is unavailable here, it is also located at `http://raspberrypigaming.com/files/QtSixA-1.5.1-src.tar.gz`.

5. Now, type `tar zxfv QtSixA-1.5.1-src.tar.gz` and press *Enter*. This will extract the contents.

6. Change to the newly created directory by typing `cd QtSixA-1.5.1-src/sixad`.

7. Now, type `make` and press *Enter*. This will turn the source code into a computer program (compiling) and will take a few minutes.

8. Next, type `sudo make install` and press *Enter*. This installs sixad into the proper locations, and allows you to run the program by typing sixad without being in a certain folder.

9. Now, type `sixad --start` and press *Enter*.

10. When prompted to press the PS key on your controller, press it. You should see a message indicating a connection to your Dual Shock.

```
pi@raspberrypi ~ $ sixad --start
sixad-bin[2585]: started
sixad-bin[2585]: sixad started, press the PS button now
sixad-bin[2585]: unable to connect to sdp session
sixad-bin[2585]: Connected Sony Computer Entertainment Wireless Controller (78:1
8:81:48:A6:62)
```

11. Press *Ctrl* + *C* to exit. Your controller will still be paired.

To pair controllers at bootup, you will need to add the sixad program to your profile. Make use of the following steps:

1. Type `nano ~/.profile` at the command line.
2. Use the arrow keys to go to the end of the file.
3. Type `sixad --start &`.
4. Press *Ctrl* + *X*, then press *Y* to save the file.
5. Now, when you log in to your Pi, sixad will automatically launch and ask to pair with your controller.

USB encoders

At the heart of every Arcade stick is a USB encoder. It takes the action of hitting a button and turns it into an input for your Raspberry Pi. Some encoders emulate a keyboard, while others act as an actual joystick. Using an encoder, you can very easily build your own customized controller.

There are hundreds of different encoders out there, but the most common ones are called the No Delay, Zero Delay, and Xin Mo board. All of these boards act as a joystick, and are very simple to wire up.

This is an example of a No Delay USB joystick encoder board. The 8 buttons are wired up to the button pins on the bottom of the board. Each button has a common and ground pin. When the button is pushed down, the connection is completed, sending the signal to the board. The joystick uses the 4 slots at the top of the board for up, down, left, and right movements. The board can also accept joysticks that only use 5 pins. Those are common with ball top sticks. The board includes a USB cable that plugs into the pins on the far-left of the board.

GPIO pins

The Raspberry Pi includes pins called GPIO that can be connected directly to a few buttons and a joystick, similar to the encoder boards we saw previously.

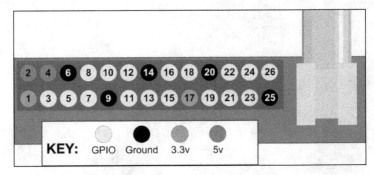

GPIO layout by raspberrypi.org

The preceding layout is of Model A and Model B. Model A+ and B+ include even more pins but are backwards compatible with the A and B pin layout. The pins we are interested in are the yellow and black-labeled pins. The other pins—1, 3, 4, and 17 are power pins. Because the buttons don't require power, we can safely ignore these. All of your buttons' ground wires should connect to a common ground pin. The other wires should individually be connected to an independent yellow GPIO pin.

While pin 8 and 10 look like proper GPIO pins, they are actually serial ports, so you should avoid using them.

Once you have connected the wires, you will need to install an application that will read from the GPIO pins and output a keyboard command.

Adafruit (http://www.adafruit.com/) has released a utility called Retrogame that does just this. It is a small C program that you can edit, then build, and run to read input from your GPIO.

By default, Retrogame has set the following controls to these pins:

Controls	Pins
Left	2
Right	3
Down	4
Up	17
Z	27
X	22

Controls	Pins
R	23
Q	18

Installing and building

To install Retrogame make use of the following steps:

1. Download Retrogame by typing `git clone https://github.com/adafruit/Adafruit-Retrogame.git` and press *Enter*.

2. Change to the new directory by typing `cd Adafruit-Retrogame`. If you need to make changes to the pin numbers or keys, type `nano retrogame.c` and scroll to around line 75. You will see a line saying **start here**. Edit the pin numbers and `KEY_` commands, as instructed.

3. Build Retrogame by typing `make retrogame` and press *Enter*.

4. When it has finished building, type `sudo ./retrogame` to test your GPIO enabled buttons.

To run it at bootup, Adafruit recommends that you add it to your `rc.local` file, as follows:

1. Type `sudo nano /etc/rc.local` and press *Enter*.

2. Go to the very last line before `exit 0`. Our entry needs to be made before this.

3. Type the path to your retrogame application, for example, `/home/pi/Adafruit-Retrogame/retrogame &`.

4. Press *Ctrl + X* and then *Y* to save the file.

5. You will now have to add a udev rule, so that other applications can see the new buttons. Udev is essentially a device manager. Setting up the rules will let other applications know how to use your device.

6. Type `sudo nano /etc/udev/rules.d/10-retrogame.rules` and press *Enter*.

7. Then, type `SUBSYSTEM=="input", ATTRS{name}=="retrogame", ENV{ID_INPUT_KEYBOARD}="1"`

8. Press *Ctrl + X*, then *Y* to save your new udev rules.

9. Now, restart your Raspberry Pi, and your GPIO controller will be ready.

Troubleshooting controllers

There are a few common problems that can crop up when using different types of controllers on your Pi. The most common one, is that you just can't seem to get your game to recognize any input. Your first step should be to check /dev/input and ensure that there is a jsX (where *x* is the joystick number) file in the directory.

```
pi@raspberrypi ~ $ cd /dev/input/
pi@raspberrypi /dev/input $ ls
by-id  by-path  event0  event1  event2  event3  event4  js0  js1  mice  mouse0
pi@raspberrypi /dev/input $
```

If you see your jsX file, type jstest /dev/input/jsX. You should now be able to press the buttons on your controller and see the different input.

```
pi@raspberrypi ~ $ jstest /dev/input/js1
Driver version is 2.1.0.
Joystick (Microsoft X-Box 360 pad) has 8 axes (X, Y, Z, Rx, Ry, Rz, HatOX, HatOY)
and 11 buttons (BtnX, BtnY, BtnTL, BtnTR, BtnTR2, BtnSelect, BtnThumbL, BtnThumbR, ?, ?, ?).
Testing ... (interrupt to exit)
Axes:  0:     0 1:     0 2:     0 3:     0 4:     0 5:     0 6:     0 7:     0 Buttons:  0:off 1
Axes:  0:     0 1:     0 2:     0 3:     0 4:     0 5:     0 6:     0 7:     0 Buttons:  0:off 1
Axes:  0:     0 1:     0 2:     0 3:     0 4:     0 5:     0 6:     0 7:     0 Buttons:  0:off 1
Axes:  0:     0 1:     0 2:     0 3:     0 4:     0 5:     0 6:     0 7:     0 Buttons:  0:off 1
Axes:  0:     0 1:     0 2:     0 3:     0 4:     0 5:     0 6:     0 7:     0 Buttons:  0:off 1
Axes:  0:     0 1:     0 2:     0 3:     0 4:     0 5:     0 6:     0 7:     0 Buttons:  0:off 1
Axes:  0:     0 1:     0 2:     0 3:     0 4:     0 5:     0 6:     0 7:     0 Buttons:  0:off 1
Axes:  0:     0 1:     0 2:     0 3:     0 4:     0 5:     0 6:     0 7:     0 Buttons:  0:off 1
Axes:  0:     0 1:     0 2:     0 3:     0 4:     0 5:     0 6:     0 7:     0 Buttons:  0:off 1
Axes:  0:     0 1:     0 2:     0 3:     0 4:     0 5:     0 6:     0 7:     0 Buttons:  0:off 1
Axes:  0: -2234 1:     0 2:     0 3:     0 4:     0 5:     0 6:     0 7:     0 Buttons:  0:off 1
Axes:  0: -2234 1:    91 2:     0 3:     0 4:     0 5:     0 6:     0 7:     0 Buttons:  0:off 1
Axes:  0: -2234 1:    91 2:-32767 3:     0 4:     0 5:     0 6:     0 7:     0 Buttons:  0:off 1
Axes:  0: -2234 1:    91 2:-32767 3:  2636 4:     0 5:     0 6:     0 7:     0 Buttons:  0:off 1
Axes:  0: -2234 1:    91 2:-32767 3:  2636 4:  -480 5:     0 6:     0 7:     0 Buttons:  0:off 1
Axes:  0: -2234 1:    91 2:-32767 3:  2636 4:  -480 5:-32767 6:     0 7:     0 Buttons:  0:off 1
Axes:  0: -2234 1:    91 2:-32767 3:  2636 4:  -480 5:-32767 6:     0 7:     0 Buttons:  0:off 1
:off 2:off 3:off 4:off 5:off 6:off 7:off 8:off 9:off 10:off
```

If you don't see anything in here, disconnect your controller, then plug it back in and run dmesg. You should see some text scroll by really quickly. The very last lines should show that you have plugged in your joystick.

If you don't see your controller in dmesg, try using a powered USB hub. Your controller might need extra power.

When running `hciconfig`, if nothing appears, it might be because your USB Bluetooth dongle isn't getting enough power. Try connecting it to a powered USB hub and see if this fixes the issue. If not, your Bluetooth dongle might not be supported.

Summary

You have now learned about different gamepads and joysticks. You have learned how to build your own, and how to connect them directly to the Raspberry Pi hardware. You also know how to connect nonstandard controllers such as the Xbox and DualShock 3. You can now troubleshoot your controllers and you have learned more about the inner workings of Raspbian and Linux.

In the next chapter, we will go over some general troubleshooting tips for the Raspberry Pi.

8
Troubleshooting

So far, we learned how to make our own game, install numerous emulators and video games, hookup peripherals, connect joysticks, and use the hardware pins. However, what happens when something goes wrong? This chapter will guide you through some of the common issues you might face with a Raspberry Pi.

Using raspi-config

The `raspi-config` tool is a basic utility that is included in each copy of Raspbian. It is a menu-based GUI that enables you to easily modify your Raspberry Pi settings.

To run `raspi-config`, type `sudo raspi-config` on the command line.

The `raspi-config` tool offers the following options:

- **Expand filesystem**: This option will resize the OS to use all of the available SD card space.

- **Change user password**: This will prompt you for a new password for the user Pi.

- **Enable boot to desktop/Scratch**: This allows you to switch between booting to the command prompt, Scratch, or the desktop.

- **Internationalization options**: This option allows you to change your time zone and your keyboard layout.

- **Enable camera**: If you have the Raspberry Pi camera module, check this to yes.

- **Add to Rastrack**: This option enables other people to know your Pi's location.

- **Overclock**: You can change your Raspberry Pi's speed here.

- **Advanced options**:

  There are many advanced options in `raspi-config` which are explained as follows:

  - **Overscan**: If you see black bars on your monitor, or your screen might be a little off; use overscan to correct it.

  - **Hostname**: This sets your Raspberry Pi's network name (Default: raspberrypi).

  - **Memory split**: This changes the memory available to the GPU, while leaving the rest to your applications. The minimum is 16 MB.

   If you have Model A or A+ the maximum split can be 192 MB, and on Model B or B+, you can go to 448 MB. I wouldn't recommend going higher than 128 MB, as you want to devote enough RAM to Linux.

  - **SSH**: This option allows you to remotely connect to your Raspberry Pi.

  - **SPI**: This enables autoloading of the SPI module. Your hardware should let you know if you need this.

  - **I2C**: This enables autoloading of the I2C module.

  - **Serial**: This option enables and disables data going to the serial pins.

  - **Audio**: This will set where audio is output from; HDMI or audio jack.

  - **Update**: This will update `raspi-config` to the latest version.

Common troubleshooting

Here are some of the common errors and the means to troubleshoot them:

EmulationStation returns an error when I try to launch it

In such a situation, run `sudo apt-get -y install libsdl1.2-dev libboost-filesystem-dev libfreeimage-dev libfreetype6-dev libsdl-mixer1.2-dev ttf-dejavu`.

This will install the required dependencies that the EmulationStation requires to run.

EmulationStation, as well as other games, might require dependencies that have not been loaded during the install. For example, `libsdl1.2-dev`, `libboost-filesystem-dev`, `libfreeimage-dev`, `libfreetype6-dev`, `libsdl-mixer1.2-dev`, and `ttf-dejavu` are common libraries that are used in a number of games that might not have been installed, or need to be updated.

Nothing happens when I apply power

In this particular instance, try out the following things:

- Make sure the power supply is rated for 5 V with at least 1 A (1000 mA). It would help if you can get up to 2.1 A (2100 mA).
- Check whether the power lights are illuminated on the board.
- Ensure that the monitor is on and plugged into the Raspberry Pi.
- Check that the SD card is formatted properly.

Most of the time, a Raspberry Pi will fail to boot, or experience problems during use, because of an inadequate power supply. Many Micro USB chargers are manufactured with minimal quality assurance, so if you do experience issues, the first thing to do would be to try a different brand of charger. Most branded cell phone chargers will properly power a Raspberry Pi.

If this doesn't fix the issue, the next step is to test out the SD card. A properly formatted SD card will have a small boot drive that is readable by Windows, Mac OS X, and Linux operating systems. If you cannot see the boot drive, or any files inside it, then it is most likely that your SD card hasn't been properly imaged.

You can also try using the NOOBS software that the Raspberry Pi Foundation offers. This is a set of files that you can drag and drop to any freshly formatted SD card. When you boot up the Raspberry Pi with that SD card, it will attempt to install an operating system onto itself. To get the NOOBS package, visit:

`http://www.raspberrypi.org/downloads/`

For more information on using NOOBS checkout:

`http://www.raspberrypi.org/introducing-noobs/`

Some of the games seem slow

You can overclock your Raspberry Pi to eke out extra performance and speed.

Warning: overclocking can corrupt your SD card, requiring you to reload Raspbian on it. If your Raspberry Pi seems to be unresponsive, reboot and hold down the *Shift* key to temporarily reset the overclock settings. Go through the following steps to overclock your Raspberry Pi:

1. Run `sudo raspi-config` from the command line.
2. Select **Overclock** from the main menu.
3. Select the lowest overclock.
4. Reboot and check the performance.
5. If it is still slow, select the next overclock setting.
6. If the game still runs at an unacceptable performance, the best bet is to post to the Raspberry Pi forums. As the Raspberry Pi platform matures, new enhancements and performance tweaks will be available.

By default, the Raspberry Pi runs at 700 MHz but has the capability to be overclocked to a higher speed. Most Raspberry Pis have been noted to be working fine at 900 MHz and some even higher than 1 GHz. Overclocking the CPU with `raspi-config` automatically throttles the speed, as required. So, when not in use, it reduces power down to 700 MHz. Even with the throttle, overclocking can make your system unstable and can lead to SD card corruption. If your system fails to boot after overclocking, holding down *Shift* tries to turn off the overclocking in the software. If this does not work, you can edit the `/boot/config.txt` file and set `arm_freq = 700` to disable overclocking. If all else fails, you can reimage your SD card. All overclocking information is stored in `config.txt`, and reimaging your card will reset it.

Connecting via HDMI doesn't work

- Edit the `config.txt` file and set `hdmi_safe = 1`.
  - Type `sudo nano /boot/config.txt`, in the terminal
  - Find the `#hdmi_safe=1` line
  - Remove the `#` from the line
  - Press *Ctrl* + *X*, then press *Y* to save the file
  - Reboot your Raspberry Pi
- Turn the TV on before turning on the Raspberry Pi.
- Try a different HDMI cable.

The *boot* drive contains a TEXT file named `config.txt`. This file stores all of the configuration parameters and is read each time your Raspberry Pi powers on. Editing this file allows you to fine-tune your Raspberry Pi and can also help resolve various issues that can crop up during use. You can also edit this file on your PC or Mac by putting the SD card into the computer.

If you have trouble getting an image to appear on your TV through HDMI, the most common fix is to edit `config.txt` and set `hdmi_safe = 1`. This changes and boosts the HDMI signal, so that it is more likely to sync with your TV. Another simple change is to ensure that the TV is on and connected before you power on the Raspberry Pi.

The DualShock 3 controller does not connect

In this case,

- Ensure that the DualShock 3 battery is fully charged.

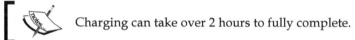 Charging can take over 2 hours to fully complete.

- Using a small pin, press the reset button on the back of the controller.
- Use a powered USB hub for your Bluetooth dongle.
- Use a Micro USB cable to ensure that the controller works when plugged in.

I get an error when compiling Retrogame

The most common cause of errors is forgetting a piece of syntax.

- Check whether each line has the proper amount of commas.
  For example: { 17,   KEY_DOWN   },

Summary

In this chapter, you have learned how to troubleshoot different ailments that can afflict your Raspberry Pi. You have learned how to overclock your processor, edit your `config.txt` to enable different modes, reset your controller, and make sure you have a proper powered Pi.

An extra piece of advice: Don't be afraid to tinker and experiment with your Raspberry Pi. It is very hard to damage the hardware. I have yet to hurt one. If everything seems broken, reformat your SD card and start over.

If all else fails, we are part of a large community of enthusiasts that want to watch you succeed. Join the forums at `http://raspberrypi.org`. There are many who will be willing to help.

Also, ensure that you check out these guides for more information:

- E-Linux Ru-Pi Troubleshooting guide at `http://elinux.org/R-Pi_Troubleshooting`
- E-Linux R-Pi Config guide at `http://elinux.org/RPiconfig`

Games List

This appendix contains of list of some of the games available from the repositories. This list is collated from the Raspberry Pi gaming subforum.

Check out the following URLs for more updates on available games:

- `http://www.raspberrypi.org/forums/viewtopic.php?f=78&t=51794`
- `http://www.raspians.com/Knowledgebase/1-debian-wheezy-games-repository-sudo-apt-get-install/`

Games available via Apt-Get

The following is the list of games that are available via Apt-Get:

- 20,000 Light Years Into Space
- 3D Chess
- 4-Digit
- Abuse
- ACM (Aliens: Colonial Marines)
- Airstrike
- Allegro demo
- Angry Drunken Dwarves
- Atom
- Atomic Tanks
- Battle for Wesnoth
- Battle Tanks
- Battleball

- Beneath a Steel Sky
- Blob Wars: Metal Blob Solid
- BlockOut 2
- DeSmuME
- Feeding Frenzy
- Flare
- Flight of the Amazon Queen
- FreeCiv
- FreeCraft
- FreeDink
- Freesweep
- Funny Boat
- Fuse
- Galaga
- Galaga: Hyperspace
- GNU Shogi
- Hexxagon
- KETM (Kill Everything That Moves)
- Lincity
- Little Crane
- Mancala
- Mednafen
- Micropolis
- Minecraft: Pi Edition
- Monsterz
- NetHack
- OpenTTD
- Overgod
- PrBoom
- Pydance
- Rafkill

- Snake4
- Sopwith
- Space Aryarya
- SpaceZero
- Spout
- Stax
- Stella
- SuperTux
- Tagua
- Teddy
- Tetzle
- TINT
- Triplane
- Vavoom
- XSoldier
- Xtron
- YahtzeeSharp

Raspberry Pi 2

As of this writing, the Raspberry Pi Foundation has introduced a brand new board called the Pi 2. While sharing the layout and price of the Model B+, the Pi 2 has been heavily upgraded.

The biggest change is the move from an ARMv6 running at 700 MHz, to a quad-core ARMv7 running at 900 MHz. The ARMv7 is a pretty big upgrade; it is what most Android releases are compiled for and the minimum version for other Linux distributions. Microsoft has even mentioned releasing a customized version of Windows 10 for the Raspberry Pi. The other major upgrade is that the RAM has been increased from 512 MB to 1 GB.

The Pi 2 is also backwards compatible with software written for the original Pi. In order to move your Pi's SD card to the newest Pi 2, follow these steps:

- On the Model A, B, or B+ run these commands:

    1. First, run the `sudo apt-get update` command.

2. After that run the `sudo apt-get upgrade` command to run the upgrades.

3. Next, run the `sudo apt-get dist-upgrade` command.

4. Finally, run the `sudo apt-get install raspberrypi-ui-mods` command.

After these tasks are completed, your operating system will be updated and you can safely move your SD card between the Pi 2 and original Raspberry Pi.

Index

PicoDrive 62
PiSNES 55, 56
Stella 63

F

FCEUX
about 55
using 55
FinalBurn Alpha
about 58
controls 64
downloading 58
URL, for downloading 58
first-person shooter (FPS) 71
Flappy Bird clone
building 19
enhancing 30
floor, creating 23-25
main character, creating 27-29
new project, creating 19
pipes, creating 26, 27
stage, setting 21, 22
variables, creating 19, 20
forever loops, Scratch 18
FreeCiv
about 81
controls 86-89
executing 82, 83
installing 82, 83
server, hosting 84-86
URL, for control list 86

G

Galaga: Hyperspace
about 93
controls 94
executing 93
installing 93
gamepads 96
games
searching, via repositories 94
Genesis/Mega Drive 62
GPIO pins
about 104
Retrogame 104

H

HDMI
connection, troubleshooting 112, 113

I

if...else statement, Scratch 18
if statement, Scratch 18
inadequate power supply
troubleshooting 111
installation
Cave Story 70
FreeCiv 82, 83
Galaga: Hyperspace 93
Mednafen, with apt-get command 54
Minecraft 76
Njam 91
NOOBS 9
Open Arena 73
PrBoom 72
Retrogame 105
Stella 63
SuperTux 89, 90
xboxdrv 98
interface, Scratch 16, 17

J

joystick package
installing 95

L

Linux
SD card, creating 9

M

Macintosh OS X
SD card, creating 8, 9
MAME4ALL
about 57
controls 65
downloading 57
URL, for downloading 57

T

troubleshooting
  controllers 106
  DualShock 3 controller connection 113
  EmulationStation execution error 110
  HDMI connection 112, 113
  inadequate power supply 111
  overclocking 112
  Retrogame compilation error 113

U

USB drive
  game controller, configuring 42
  used, for copying game files onto Pi 48
USB encoders 102, 103

V

variable, Scratch 18

W

Wi-Fi access point
  Raspberry Pi, connecting to 10-13
Wi-Fi adapter
  URL 13
Win32DiskImager
  about 7
  URL 7
Windows
  SD card, creating 7, 8

X

Xbox 360 controllers 98
xboxdrv
  about 98
  installing 98
  using 99

Thank you for buying
Raspberry Pi Gaming
Second Edition

About Packt Publishing

Packt, pronounced 'packed', published its first book, *Mastering phpMyAdmin for Effective MySQL Management*, in April 2004, and subsequently continued to specialize in publishing highly focused books on specific technologies and solutions.

Our books and publications share the experiences of your fellow IT professionals in adapting and customizing today's systems, applications, and frameworks. Our solution-based books give you the knowledge and power to customize the software and technologies you're using to get the job done. Packt books are more specific and less general than the IT books you have seen in the past. Our unique business model allows us to bring you more focused information, giving you more of what you need to know, and less of what you don't.

Packt is a modern yet unique publishing company that focuses on producing quality, cutting-edge books for communities of developers, administrators, and newbies alike. For more information, please visit our website at www.packtpub.com.

Writing for Packt

We welcome all inquiries from people who are interested in authoring. Book proposals should be sent to author@packtpub.com. If your book idea is still at an early stage and you would like to discuss it first before writing a formal book proposal, then please contact us; one of our commissioning editors will get in touch with you.

We're not just looking for published authors; if you have strong technical skills but no writing experience, our experienced editors can help you develop a writing career, or simply get some additional reward for your expertise.

Raspberry Pi Cookbook for Python Programmers

ISBN: 978-1-84969-662-3   Paperback: 402 pages

Over 50 easy-to-comprehend tailor-made recipes to get the most out of the Raspberry Pi and unleash its huge potential using Python

1. Install your first operating system, share files over the network, and run programs remotely.

2. Unleash the hidden potential of the Raspberry Pi's powerful Video Core IV graphics processor with your own hardware accelerated 3D graphics.

3. Discover how to create your own electronic circuits to interact with the Raspberry Pi.

Raspberry Pi Robotic Projects

ISBN: 978-1-84969-432-2   Paperback: 278 pages

Create amazing robotic projects on a shoestring budget

1. Make your projects talk and understand speech with Raspberry Pi.

2. Use standard webcam to make your projects see and enhance vision capabilities.

3. Full of simple, easy-to-understand instructions to bring your Raspberry Pi online for developing robotics projects.

Please check **www.PacktPub.com** for information on our titles

Raspberry Pi Server Essentials

ISBN: 978-1-78328-469-6   Paperback: 116 pages

Transform your Raspberry Pi into a server for hosting websites, games, or even your Bitcoin network

1. Unlock the various possibilities of using Raspberry Pi as a server.

2. Configure a media center for your home or sharing with friends.

3. Connect to the Bitcoin network and manage your wallet.

Raspberry Pi Super Cluster

ISBN: 978-1-78328-619-5   Paperback: 126 pages

Build your own parallel-computing cluster using Raspberry Pi in the comfort of your home

1. Learn about parallel computing by building your own system using Raspberry Pi.

2. Build a two-node parallel computing cluster.

3. Integrate Raspberry Pi with Hadoop to build your own super cluster.

Please check **www.PacktPub.com** for information on our titles